Who Benefits from Government Expenditure?

A Case Study of Colombia

A World Bank Research Publication

Who Benefits from Government Expenditure?

A Case Study of Colombia

Marcelo Selowsky

Published for the World Bank
Oxford University Press

Oxford University Press

NEW YORK OXFORD LONDON GLASGOW
TORONTO MELBOURNE WELLINGTON HONG KONG
TOKYO KUALA LUMPUR SINGAPORE JAKARTA
DELHI BOMBAY CALCUTTA MADRAS KARACHI
NAIROBI DAR ES SALAAM CAPE TOWN

© 1979 by the International Bank
for Reconstruction and Development / The World Bank
1818 H Street, N.W., Washington, D.C. 20433 U.S.A.

The views and interpretations in this book are the
author's and should not be attributed to the World
Bank, to its affiliated organizations, or to any
individual acting in their behalf.

Library of Congress Cataloging in Publication Data
Selowsky, Marcelo.
 Who benefits from government expenditure?
 Bibliography: p. 180
 Includes index.
 1. Colombia—Appropriations and expenditures.
2. Income distribution—Colombia. I. International
Bank for Reconstruction and Development. II. Title.
HJ2083.S44   336.861   79-16384
ISBN 0-19-520098-5
ISBN 0-19-520099-3 pbk.

Contents

Figures

Tables

Foreword

THIS STUDY OF COLOMBIA by Marcelo Selowsky and the companion study of Malaysia by Jacob Meerman were undertaken in 1974 as complements to other work of the World Bank on income distribution. They were undertaken in recognition of the fact that the welfare of the poor is affected not only by their income, narrowly defined, but also by the services that they receive from their governments. By now the notion of basic needs is commonplace; attributes of systems for meeting these needs—such as accessibility, reasonable prices, and cost effectiveness—are well known. Consequently, the idea of using specially designed household surveys to investigate the distribution of public expenditure and to explain it to some extent may seem less novel than it did five years ago.

It is not unusual for the Bank to undertake research of an experimental nature in the hope that others will be able to make use of both the results and the experience gained in attaining the results. In this instance both authors advocate similar investigations in other countries, not only as a one-time effort in each country, but also at intervals of from five to ten years to monitor progress. In essence, this is a plea that governments build on the initial efforts of these authors and institutionalize them.

One thing which emerges clearly from the studies, however, is the great difficulty—sometimes the impossibility—of extracting significant complementary information from government accounts, even good ones. On reflection this is not too surprising, since government fiscal systems are not designed originally as information systems. Governments that command large shares of the national products of their countries and wish to use them efficiently for clearly specified objectives may well need to exploit more fully their untapped sources of information. The value of these studies today rests on their intrinsic merit, but their potential value may be much greater by virtue of their demonstration effect.

BENJAMIN B. KING
Director, Development Economics Department
The World Bank

June 1979
Washington, D.C.

Acknowledgments

I AM INDEBTED to several individuals and institutions for making this research possible. Jaime H. Caro, Carlos Lemoine, and Francisco Pereira contributed to the sample survey design and were central in planning the earlier stages of the study. COLDATOS (Compañia Colombiana de Datos) carried out the field work for the survey and the initial work on data processing. DANE (Departamento de Estadística) and INPES (Instituto para Programas Especiales de la Salud) provided data on the education and health sector that were crucial in analyzing the distribution of public expenditure in these sectors. Earlier discussions with researchers of CEDE (Universidad de Los Andes), as well as with Ricardo Galan, Jacob Meerman, Manuel Ramírez, and Miguel Urrutia were extremely useful in planning the research. Finally, I am indebted to Mariene Lehwing and Zaitun Virji for valuable research assistance and to Aludia Oropesa for typing the final manuscript.

Nancy W. Donovan edited an early draft, and Virginia deHaven Orr edited the final manuscript. Brian J. Svikhart directed design and production, Florence Robinson indexed the text, and Carol Crosby Black designed the cover.

MARCELO SELOWSKY

Who Benefits from Government Expenditure?

A Case Study of Colombia

Introduction and Summary

ONE POLICY OPTION OPEN TO GOVERNMENTS to improve the distribution of income and to eradicate extreme poverty is to change the composition and direction of public expenditure. This option now has an important potential in most developing countries for two reasons.

First, government expenditure has become a significant fraction of national income. The present information available on the personal distribution of income indicates that this expenditure is also quite large compared with the share of national income received by the poorest groups of the population. Hence, changes in the direction of this expenditure can have a significant effect on the real income of the lowest income groups: in a country where government expenditure and the income of the poorest 20 percent of the population account for 25 and 5 percent, respectively, of the gross national product (GNP), reallocating 10 percent of the fiscal budget to this group would increase its income by 50 percent. Such a reallocation is one of the most feasible options from a political point of view. It does not represent an important trade-off with the growth rate; even if half of it were to be made at the expense of public investment and assuming that no assets would be created in the poorest group, the growth rate of GNP would decline only 0.25 percentage points.[1]

Second, and more important than the capacity to transfer income, is the use of the fiscal budget to increase the consumption of specific goods and services. Not only per capita income is dis-

1. Assuming a social return to capital of 0.20, the growth rate of the GNP would diminish by $(0.0125)(0.20) = 0.0025$.

3

tributed unequally; this is also true for other welfare indicators—such as life expectancy, calorie consumption, and minimum literacy—that by now have become goals on their own. This situation reflects an inequality in the consumption of food and services, such as housing, water, sewerage, education, and health. Policies to increase their consumption above the levels resulting from the regular forces of supply and demand define what has become known as a "basic needs" approach to poverty alleviation. The notion is to use the fiscal budget to direct the allocation of resources to reach these critical levels of consumption at earlier stages of development: that is, earlier than would have been reached in the normal growth of per capita income. The argument becomes more important in three circumstances: (a) the smaller the trickle down effect of GNP growth on the income of the poor; (b) the smaller the marginal propensity of the poor to spend on "basic needs;" and (c) the smaller the possibility of the private sector supplying these services because of complementarities and economies of scale in these sectors.

What is the present performance of developing countries in reaching the poorest income groups through public expenditure? How has this performance evolved over time? Are there constraints on the consumption of these services other than the mere availability or supply of these services? This research study addresses these questions with the help of a case study; the country selected is Colombia.

Methodology

A full evaluation of the distributive effect of government expenditure would require a model to predict the effect of this expenditure on each income group, as owners of factors of production and as consumers of final goods and services. Such a model would involve specifying most factor and commodity markets and would have to be highly complex, such as a general equilibrium model.

The objectives of this study, however, are less ambitious. It concentrates on the publicly provided services whose consumption by individuals or households can be identified and measured. This approach omits the typical "public good," such as defense and justice. It measures the consumption of public services as a final commodity, rather than tracing the distributive effect when the services are consumed as a factor of production.

Specifically this study identifies the beneficiaries of publicly provided services, measures the subsidy received by households from consuming some of these services, and attempts to explain the present distribution of consumption in terms of supply and demand: that is, to what extent is the absence of consumption of particular services the result of the unavailability of supply and to what extent is it the result of demand factors governing the utilization of such supply?

For this purpose a specifically designed country-wide survey of 4,019 households in Colombia was carried out in November 1974. The survey data are classified by rural and urban location, and the urban data are classified further according to city size. The survey provides household income data that are used to classify the beneficiaries of government services in the overall distribution of income.

Results

The survey was able to trace the beneficiaries of one-third of total government expenditure. The major expenditures accounting for this fraction are the public subsidies to the education and health sector and the investment in electricity, water, and sewerage.

The total subsidy to education is distributed evenly across income quintiles: that is, the subsidy per household is constant across income groups. It results, however, from different subsidies to each educational level. The subsidy to primary education is progressive, whereas the subsidy to higher education is highly regressive; actually it is more unequally distributed than personal income. The health subsidy is also relatively similar across households, although it varies according to the source: The National Health System has a progressive effect, whereas the Social Security System network favors the middle-income quintiles. The relative constancy of the subsidy per household across income groups does not hold when it is expressed in per capita terms. The reason for this is the difference in family size in each per capita income group. The poorest quintile of households accounts for 25.1 percent of the population, whereas the richest accounts for 15.4 percent, a difference of 60 percent in family size. The per capita subsidy to the richest quintile becomes 1.6 times larger than that to the poorest quintile.

For electricity, water, and sewerage, data were obtained on the distribution of households who had the service in 1974 and who received the service between 1970 and 1974. A comparison of the figures indicates the distributive direction of investment in those sectors over time.

The distribution of beneficiaries by quintiles in 1974 is quite similar across services. Between 25 and 30 percent of the households with services belong to the bottom 40 percent of households, whereas 50 to 55 percent belong to the upper 40 percent. Almost all consumers are concentrated in urban areas. The fact that low-income quintiles consume less of these services is more a result of those services being concentrated in urban areas—rural households being relatively poorer in the country distribution of income—than an intra-urban discrimination against low-income groups. The distribution of new beneficiaries is much more progressive. New investment in these sectors has been more redistributive than in the past. Part of this change results from the fact that investment had a lower "urban bias:" that is, a large fraction of the new beneficiaries have been rural households, particularly for electricity and piped water. Within the urban sector investment has also tended increasingly to benefit poorer households.

What factors explain the distribution of consumption of electricity, water, and sewerage services? A multivariate analysis was carried out to identify variables associated with the consumption of these services by urban households. A framework was developed where this association could be interpreted as a relation of causality. A situation in which the household does not use the service because of inaccessability (the supply network is too far) is distinguished from a situation where demand factors constrain the use of that supply. The Colombia data suggest that half of the urban households without the service fall in the latter category. Therefore the study made a special effort to identify the extent to which variables such as per capita income, education, and migrant status affect the probability of a household demanding the service.

The survey also identified the beneficiaries of other services and subsidies: street lighting and garbage collection services, educational fellowships, adult retraining courses at SENA (the Colombian Retraining Center), and the subsidy embodied in the loans from the Caja Agraria, the main public agency channeling subsidized credit to farmers. Although they are less important as a fraction of total government expenditure, the effect of these services and subsidies on particular groups can be important.

The survey was unable to identify the beneficiaries of investment in roads, a large item of public investment in Colombia. Questions regarding changes in the mode and time of travel did not yield significant results. Either investment in roads has basically a benefit as an intermediate input—instead of as a consumer good—or the questionnaire method used was not the proper technique to measure the benefit of this type of service.

Conclusions

This research, initially conceived as a pilot study, shows that specifically designed household surveys can provide relatively good information on the distributive direction of a large portion of government expenditure. Ideally such a survey should be repeated —for example, every five years—to capture the distributive direction of investment and changing government programs. Accordingly, the design of the survey questionnaire should be adjusted continuously to identify the beneficiaries of new kinds of programs. The advantage of a countrywide survey of this kind is the information it provides on households not consuming particular services. From a policy point of view, it is fundamental to determine whether this situation results from a lack of supply of the service or from demand phenomena governing the use of that supply.

Chapter I

Background and Main Results

To IDENTIFY THE SPECIFIC POLICY OPTIONS that can be used to change the composition and direction of public expenditure, the distributive direction of the present public expenditure first must be evaluated. This study makes such an evaluation with the help of a case study. Colombia was the country chosen for the study; it represents the typical middle-income ($600 per capita income), semi-industrialized Latin American country.[1] It has a growing urban population, strong income differences between regions, and both commercial and small subsistence farming. The data base is reasonably good, and earlier work on the subject allows comparison of results.[2]

Objectives and Limitations

A full evaluation of the distributive effect of government expenditure—the change in the real income of individuals resulting from the total or marginal presence of the government—is beyond the scope of this research, since it would require a model of the determinants of the incidence of government intervention through factor and final goods markets. When this intervention provides public services whose benefits may not be completely internalized

---

1. Throughout the text, "dollar" ($) refers to U.S. dollar.
2. The most comprehensive survey of past research on income distribution is Albert Berry and Miguel Urrutia, *Income Distribution in Colombia* (New Haven: Yale University Press, 1967).

in market demands (for example, health), an additional difficulty arises. The benefits from the extra consumption of these services cannot be approximated by the prices individuals were paying for private substitutes before public intervention. Thus, tracing such benefits becomes a problem analogous to that in social project evaluation.

This study addresses a more restricted set of questions, which can be summarized as follows:

- *How is the consumption of publicly provided services distributed by income groups, regions, and other relevant characteristics associated with income levels?*

This study only covers services for which individual or household consumption can be identified and, if possible, measured. The typical pure public good, such as defense or justice, is excluded.

- *What is the subsidy associated with the provision of these services by the public sector?*

Two definitions of the subsidy are of interest. The first definition is the subsidy derived from the government pricing policy: in other words, the difference between the long-run cost of the service to the government and the price to consumers. It takes the presence of the public sector as given and simply asks about the distributive effect of the government pricing policy. The second definition is the subsidy of having a public sector with that particular pricing policy as opposed to a situation in which equivalent services would have been provided by the private sector. This subsidy consists of the earlier definition (the pricing policy subsidy) plus the difference in cost between private and public provision of the service.

For particular services, this research derives estimates for the first definition of the subsidy. Estimates for the second definition would require data on the cost of equivalent services in the absence of public intervention (for example, the cost to a household of obtaining a unit of light from oil lamps)—a task beyond the scope of this study.

- *What factors explain the distribution of consumption addressed in the first question? How much can be explained by the existing structure of supply of the service and how much by factors governing the private demand for these services?*

This is a difficult area to research. It is, however, the most relevant in identifying policy instruments to increase the consumption of these services by low-income groups.

To identify these policy instruments, it is useful to distinguish between two types of situations in which a particular household does not consume a public service: (1) the household does not consume the service because the supply network is not geographically present and (2) the household is on the supply network but decides not to consume the service.

In the first instance there is no consumption because of the location of the supply network: it is basically an institutional datum determined by past investment decisions in the sector. In the second, the lack of consumption is determined by demand and results from a voluntary choice. Because the factors governing this choice (variables behind the demand) may be different from the factors determining the location of the network (variables behind the supply), it is useful to recognize explicitly this supply-demand mechanism behind consumption. This study attempts to identify the explanatory factors behind the supply and demand for particular services.

• *What income groups have benefited from the changes in the supply of these services as a result of recent investment policies?*

Thus far, the research has addressed the distribution of consumption at one time: that is, the consumption stemming from the existing supply or stock of infrastructure. Of at least equal interest is the distribution of new consumers of the service that results from expansions of the supply over time. For those sectors in which investment has been significant as a fraction of the national budget, this study estimates the income distribution of the new households consuming the service.

Methodology and Further Simplifications

This section outlines the methodology followed to address the four questions stated above. It will become evident that further simplifications are required in addition to those already mentioned.

The subsidy received by a household from consuming a service (S) is equal to the subsidy per unit (s) multiplied by the units of that service being consumed by the household (Q). The subsidy per unit is equal to the difference between the long-run marginal cost to the government of providing the service (c) and the price charged to consumers (p). The quantity consumed (Q) is itself a function of the price charged and of other socioeconomic variables (x) influencing the household demand for the service.[3]

3. The relation between the two definitions of the subsidy discussed earlier and the extra benefits to consumers out of public provision of the service are shown in the figure below.

Suppose D is the demand for the service and c and c' are the long-run marginal costs of providing the service by the public and by the private sector, respectively. Assume further that c' is greater than c (the public provision has a lower cost than the private substitute) and that the government prices the service at p, below its cost, c.

The implicit subsidy of having the service provided by the public sector with that pricing policy—instead of by the private sector—is equal to $s^* = s + \Delta c$; s^* is therefore equal to the pure pricing policy subsidy (the definition to be used in this study) plus the difference in cost between provision by the private and by the public sector.

The extra consumer surplus resulting from public provision of the service—when it replaces more expensive private sources of the service—is $s^* [Q_0 + \frac{1}{2} (Q_2 - Q_0)]$. The one resulting from the pure pricing policy is equal to $s [Q_1 + \frac{1}{2} (Q_2 - Q_1)]$. The concept of S used in this study is $S = sQ_2$.

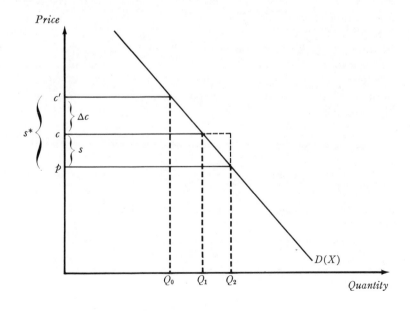

The problem of using the national budget to identify public services with significant subsidies and the limitations of using the budget to compute c, the long-run cost of providing these services, are discussed first. The household sample survey carried out to derive data on the Q_is and to identify the factors influencing consumption is then described.

Identification of public services through the national budget

Public services can be thought of as a flow of services provided by a capital stock (or stock of infrastructure) and other variable resources such as labor and intermediate inputs. The long-run marginal cost of a unit of this flow includes the opportunity cost of capital required to provide this unit plus the associated variable cost.

To what extent does the government budget provide a measure for this long-run marginal cost? If the public sector hired or rented the capital stock or infrastructure from the private sector, the annual rental payments that would appear in the national budget could be used for this purpose. Since the public sector owns the stock, no rental payments are recorded in the budget. Only non-rental or running costs, that is, labor services and intermediate inputs, appear explicitly. The more labor intensive the production of a public service is, the more easily the long-run cost can be approximated by the cost data in the national budget.

The extreme, though not uncommon, example is that of a capital-intensive public service with negligible labor and intermediate input cost, for example, electricity derived from hydro sources. The national budget is unable to capture the true marginal cost of providing the service during a particular year. This cost can only be estimated from micro studies of an expansion of the given system.

The empirical implications of this are quite clear. By using the government's current expenditures as a substitute for the cost of the service, only the labor-intensive public services, that is, education and health, can be examined. Consequently this study derives subsidy figures for these sectors only. The estimated figures will understate the true subsidy received by households to the extent that the rental cost of the capital stock in these sectors is not included in the budget.

No estimates are presented here for subsidies to capital-intensive public services.[4] In the case of electricity, piped water, and sewerage, availability at one time and the supply-demand mechanism behind consumption are analyzed, and the income groups that benefited from expansions in the supply network over time are identified.

Some attempts were made to estimate the benefits of investment in roads, an important fraction of the national budget in Colombia. The mechanism by which this investment generates benefits, however, proved too complex to be measured by a household survey.

A different problem arises in dealing with the health services provided by the social security system for employees in the private sector. This system is financed largely by contributions from private employers and employees, with a minimal contribution from the central government. Although the measured contribution from the public sector is small, the system induces an important transfer across income groups. Because the size of the transfer depends on the real or economic incidence induced by the legal contributions, a simple labor market model was developed in Chapter 4 to derive this incidence.

The 1974 household sample survey

Two possible strategies can be followed to derive data on the consumption of public services by income groups. First, household income data can be taken from the records of the institutions that provide the services. If these records do not contain income data, this information can be obtained by interviewing a sample of households listed in those records. Second, a countrywide sample survey can be made, including households with and without services.

Given the objectives of this study, the countrywide survey has two main advantages. First, it provides data on households without services. From a policy point of view, this information is more important than data on the distribution of households with services. Second, it generates its own income distribution data against

---

4. Some estimates of the transfer across consumers resulting from the tariff structure for electricity and water are presented in the appendix to Chapter 5.

which to map the households to be studied; this makes it unnecessary to use income distribution estimates from other sources and thus avoids problems of comparability.

TRADEOFFS IN THE SAMPLE DESIGN. To address simultaneously the four questions stated above implies a tradeoff in the sample design. If the objective is to derive a statistically significant estimate for the income groups already consuming services, a minimum sample size breakdown for these groups is required. If the emphasis is on income groups without services or on ones that have only recently received them, a minimum sample size of low-income groups is necessary.

This tradeoff becomes particularly important in testing the factors behind the availability of services in a supply-demand context. For such an analysis, a minimum sample size of households without services is needed to split the group further between those who are on the supply network and those who are not. Since public services are available in most of the urban areas in Colombia, low-income groups must be overrepresented in the sample to obtain a minimum sample size of households without services. This problem will be considered again in the discussion of the results.

A sample survey of 4,019 households and 22,064 individuals was undertaken especially for this study by the Compañía Colombiana de Datos (COLDATOS) in December 1974.[5] The composition of the sample according to major breakdowns appears in Table 1.1.

STRATIFICATION. Urbanization, as measured by city size, is the first level of stratification used in the sample design. This stratification results from two hypotheses. The first is that urbanization is highly correlated with the consumption of government services. Thus, the first requirement in the stratification is to provide statistically significant estimates for major urban strata classified by city size. The second hypothesis is that the higher the degree of urbanization, the more the consumption of services varies across households, this variation being associated with the level of household income. The second requirement, therefore, is to derive sig-

---

5. A full description of the sample design and stratification can be found in Compañía Colombiana de Datos (COLDATOS) "Diseño de la Muestra del Banco Mundial" (study prepared for the World Bank, Bogotá, 1976; processed).

Table 1.1. *Size and Major Categories of the 1974 Sample Survey*

Major regions (inhabitants)	Strata	Selected neighbor- hoods or hamlets	Selected households	Percentage of households	
				In the sample	In the population
Large cities	5[a,b]	184	1050	26.2	28.9
(more than 500,000)[a]		(neighbor- hoods)			
	(1)	(51)	(321)	(8.0)	(3.2)
	(2)	(70)	(355)	(8.9)	(11.3)
	(3)	(40)	(203)	(5.1)	(10.1)
	(4)	(17)	(94)	(2.3)	(2.2)
	(5)	(6)	(77)	(1.9)	(2.1)
Intermediate cities	9	187	994	24.7	17.5
(30,000 to 500,000)		(neighbor- hoods)			
Small towns	13	13	725	18.0	15.5
(1,500 to 30,000)		(cities)			
Rural areas	21	114	1,250	31.1	38.1
(less than 1,500)					
Total	48	498	4,019	100.0	100.0

a. "Large cities" include Bogotá, Cali, Medellín, and Barranquilla.
b. The five strata in the large cities are defined as follows: (1) slum neighborhoods; (2) low-income neighborhoods; (3) low-middle- and middle-income neighborhoods; (4) middle-high- and high-income neighborhoods; and (5) municipalities attached to the large metropolitan areas. These definitions of strata are taken from the sample frame of neighborhoods used by the Bureau of Census (see the appendix to this chapter).

nificant estimates of consumption by major income or socioeconomic groups, at least for the largest cities.

The first regional breakdown of the sample is urban-rural, with the urban population classified by city size according to three major categories: large cities of over 500,000 inhabitants (the four largest in Colombia); intermediate cities of 30,000 to 500,000 inhabitants; and small towns of 1,500 to 30,000 inhabitants. These four major categories are broken down further into forty-eight strata: five for large cities, nine for intermediate cities, thirteen for small towns, and twenty-one for the rural areas.

Each of the five strata in the large cities defines a group of neighborhoods with homogeneous socioeconomic characteristics. The geographic definitions of the neighborhoods are taken from urban maps, and their characteristics are derived from the 1970 household survey undertaken by the Bureau of Census (Departamento de Estadística; DANE).[6] A total of 184 neighborhoods or clusters are selected from these strata.

Intermediate cities are grouped into nine strata, with each group defined according to major geographic region and city size (between 30,000 and 100,000 and between 100,000 and 500,000 inhabitants). From each stratum one city is selected. Three criteria are used to classify the small towns: a further breakdown of the size of towns, geographic region (as described above), and characteristics of the agricultural activities surrounding the town. One town is selected from each stratum.

The twenty-one rural strata are derived from the aggregation of 786 micro-rural regions or primary sampling units (PSU) that had been defined previously according to several criteria of agricultural homogeneity.[7] One or two PSU are chosen from each of the twenty-one strata, three to eight hamlets are selected from each PSU, and ten to twelve dwellings from each hamlet.

DISTRIBUTION OF HOUSEHOLDS BY INCOME QUINTILES. Table 1.2 shows the composition of the sample after the survey had been carried out and the household income data computed. The distribution of households in the population is obtained by expanding the household data according to the weights derived from the stratification procedure, which corrects for any under- or overrepresentation in the sample. The expanded or weighted data can then be used to derive the distribution of households in different regions according to per capita household income. It is also possible to order households in each region according to per capita income and to compute the income figures that define quintiles (fifths) of the total population or households in the region.

Table 1.2 also presents the number of sampled households in each of the income ranges defining quintiles. This information provides the basis for judging whether the initial objective of the stratification—overrepresentation of low-income groups—was

---

6. See the appendix to this chapter.

7. Each PSU includes one to three adjacent municipalities with the same access road and similar agricultural activities. These activities were defined as: cattle raising; coffee growing; large agro-industrialized farming (sugar, cotton); and cropping activities (for example, corn and yucca) in subsistence farming. For a detailed description, see the COLDATOS report.

Table 1.2. *Number of Households in the Sample,*
Classified by Quintiles
in the (Expanded) Regional Distribution of Income

Income quintile (poorest to richest)[a]	Large cities	Inter- mediate cities	Small towns	Urban total	Rural areas	Country total
1	285	208	137	663	278	863
2	259	227	155	624	261	886
3	209	188	145	567	239	796
4	152	198	150	499	252	786
5	145	173	138	416	220	688
Country total	1,050	994	725	2,769	1,250	4,019

a. Quintiles are calculated from the weighted number of households in the income levels in each region. Because the per capita household income defining a particular quintile differs from region to region, figures in a row do not necessarily add up to urban or to country totals.

achieved. If the share of households sampled in one quintile is larger than 20 percent (the share in the population), that quintile is overrepresented in the sample. The table shows that this is indeed the case for low-income groups, particularly those in the largest cities.

Main Results

The main results of this study are presented in this section. Thus, it is possible to compare the distribution of beneficiaries across all the public services studied. The distributions for each service are presented and analyzed in detail in separate chapters.

Distribution of income

The income data from the survey can be used to estimate the distribution of income in both urban and rural areas. Such estimates are given in Table 1.3, which presents urban, rural, and countrywide income distribution data. Results are shown for the accumulated percentages of families, in ascending order according to household per capita income. For each accumulated percentage of families, the corresponding accumulated percentage of individuals and the accumulated share of the total income is given. For example, the poorest 40 percent of urban households make up 46.9

Table 1.3. *Distribution of Income, 1974*
(accumulated percentages)

Percentage of house-holds, by per capita household income (lowest to highest)	Urban		Rural[a]		Country	
	Popu-lation	Income	Popu-lation	Income	Popu-lation	Income
10	12.5	1.7	13.4	3.0	13.0	1.9
20	24.7	4.6	24.9	7.6	25.1	5.2
30	36.2	8.6	36.6	13.8	36.5	9.4
40	46.9	13.3	47.7	20.9	47.2	14.3
50	56.8	18.9	59.2	29.8	57.7	20.4
60	66.1	25.5	68.6	38.6	66.9	26.9
70	75.5	34.2	76.7	47.5	75.7	34.9
80	84.4	45.7	85.5	59.4	84.4	45.6
90	92.6	62.3	93.5	73.5	92.5	60.7
95	98.5	73.9	97.0	81.9	96.4	72.8

a. Population living in conglomerates of less than 1,500 inhabitants.

percent of the urban population and receive 13.3 percent of the total urban income.

The data suggest that rural income is more evenly distributed, particularly at low levels of income, even if reference is made to the distribution of the population instead of to the distribution of households. This is contrary to estimates for 1964 by Berry and Urrutia, although it can be partly explained by the fact that their estimates included the income of landowners living in cities in the rural income figure.[8]

A comparison of Gini coefficients from the 1974 sample survey and from Berry and Urrutia yields the following figures:

	Gini coefficients		
	Urban	Rural	Country
Berry and Urrutia (1964) (economically active population)	0.55	0.57	0.57
1974 Sample survey			
Population	0.54	0.42	0.50
Households	0.48	0.32	0.47

8. Berry and Urrutia, *Income Distribution in Colombia*, Chapter 2.

Figure 1.1. *Distribution of Income:*
Comparison of Estimates

Percent of income

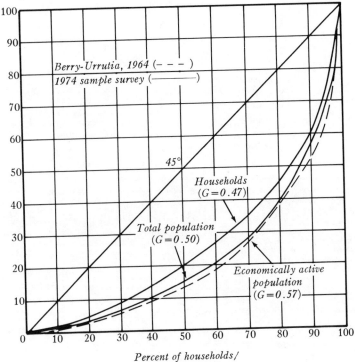

Percent of households/
Percent of population

Because low-income groups have a larger family size, the Gini coefficient for the distribution of the population is larger than for the distribution of households. Although the estimate for the urban population is almost the same as that of Berry and Urrutia, the difference between the estimates is substantial for rural areas.

A comparison of Lorenz curves for the total country is presented for both estimates in Figure 1.1. The curves for the urban areas are quite similar if the distribution of the population is used for the sample survey figures.

The same income data can be used to compute the fraction of

Table 1.4. *Per Capita Income Conversions, November 1974*

	Monthly per capita income (pesos)	
Annual per capita income (dollars)	According to the official exchange rate = 27.6 pesos	According to the Kravis parity for private consumption = 13.0 pesos[a]
0–50	0–115	0–54
51–75	116–172	55–81
76–100	173–230	82–108
101–150	231–345	109–162
151–250	346–575	163–271
251–350	576–805	272–379
351–500	806–1,150	380–542
501–700	1,151–1,610	543–758
701–1,500	1,611–3,450	759–1,625
Over 1,500	Over 3,450	Over 1,625

a. This parity was calculated on the basis of 8.3 pesos for 1970. The parity for November 1974 becomes equal to:

$$8.3 \left[1 + (\Delta p/p)_{Col}/1 + (\Delta p/p)_{US} \right] = 8.3 \, (2.09/1.33) = 13.0$$

where $\Delta p/p$ corresponds to the change in the price level between 1970 and November 1974 in Colombia and the United States. Irving B. Kravis, Zoltan Kenessey, Alan Heston, and Robert Summers, *A System of International Comparisons of Gross Product and Purchasing Power* (Baltimore: Johns Hopkins University Press for the World Bank, 1975).

the population receiving a per capita income lower than a predetermined value, such as a poverty cutoff line. To derive that information for predetermined values of per capita income in dollars (to facilitate international comparisons), an exchange rate is required. Two alternative values can be used for November 1974 (a month before the survey): the official exchange rate of 27.6 pesos to the dollar and the Kravis parity rate for private consumption of 13 pesos to the dollar. In Table 1.4 the monthly per capita income in Colombian pesos, equal to predetermined ranges of dollar annual per capita income, is shown for both exchange rates.[9]

9. Table 1.4 was calculated from data on the distribution of households by per capita income according to both exchange rates. These data are presented in the statistical appendix, Tables SA-1 and SA-2.

Table 1.5. *Percent of Households below Poverty Lines*

Annual per capita income (dollars)	Urban		Rural		Country	
	Official rate	Kravis rate	Official rate	Kravis rate	Official rate	Kravis rate
Below 50	5.9	1.4	10.5	1.9	7.6	1.6
Below 100	20.8	5.3	37.0	9.6	26.8	7.0
Below 150	35.9	11.3	60.0	21.0	44.8	15.0

Table 1.5 shows the percentage of households in each region below commonly used poverty lines: that is, with per capita yearly incomes of less than $50, $100, and $150. As expected, the results are extremely sensitive to the choice of exchange rates. Calculated with the Kravis rate, the percent of households with a per capita income under $50 is negligible; below $100, it is a fourth of what it would be if the official exchange rate were used.

Education and health

In 1974 the total public subsidy to education, which includes the cost of public education plus subsidies to private schools, was 11.2 percent of the total public expenditure and 2.2 percent of the GNP. The estimated public subsidy to health was 3.6 percent of the total public expenditure and 0.7 percent of the GNP, or approximately one-third of the subsidy to education. As noted previously, these estimates do not include the opportunity cost of the public capital stock in these sectors.

Colombia's health system consists of institutions belonging to the National Health System (NHS), which theoretically benefits all individuals; institutions maintained by the Social Security of the Public Sector (Cajas Publicas), with which employees in the public sector are affiliated; and institutions run by the Colombian Institute of Social Security (ICSS), with which employees in the private sector are affiliated.

In their running costs, the NHS and ICSS are of similar size, and together they account for approximately 90 percent of the running cost of the entire health network. Nevertheless, a different

Table 1.6. *Distribution of Subsidies for Education and Health per Household and per Capita, Classified by Income Quintile* (1974 pesos)

Income quintile (poorest to richest)	Subsidy for education				Subsidy for health		
	Primary	Secondary	University	Total	NHS	SSS	Total
1	1,305	598	18	1,921	514	103	617
2	1,089	776	96	1,961	440	186	626
3	835	751	224	1,810	393	381	774
4	589	872	489	1,950	321	314	635
5	252	555	1,257	2,064	210	295	505
Country average	816	718	413	1,947	376	255	631

strategy is required to compute the subsidy received by the beneficiaries of the two systems. The subsidy to the NHS is relatively easy to compute because it is directly financed by the Ministry of Health and by contributions from the departmental governments. The ICSS subsidy comes from workers and employers in the private sector, whose contributions amount to 95 percent of the total financing.

The implicit subsidy received by the ICSS affiliates is equal to the total contributions to the system minus the real incidence borne by labor. The share borne by labor is equal to the difference between the present wage and the wage that would have prevailed without the system. This share depends not only on legal (percentage) contributions and on the supply and demand elasticities for labor, but also on the value placed by workers on the yearly services provided by the system, which affects the new (post-system) supply price of labor and therefore the new equilibrium wage.

It is estimated here that half of the total financing of the system is borne by labor. This figure is higher than the legal incidence of 0.33 resulting from legal rates of 3.5 and 7 percent of the wage that is paid by workers and employers, respectively $(0.035/0.105 = 0.33)$.

Total subsidies for education and health	Mean household size (persons)	Subsidy per capita		Annual household income	Subsidy as a percentage of household income
		1974 pesos	1974 US$		
2,538	6.87	369	13.3	10,368	24.5
2,587	5.99	436	15.6	17,820	14.5
2,584	5.38	480	17.4	25,032	10.3
2,585	4.80	539	19.5	36,912	7.0
2,569	4.25	604	21.9	104,388	2.5
2,578	5.50	468	17.0	38,904	6.6

Table 1.6 presents estimates of the subsidy received by the representative household in each income quintile. These quintiles are defined by the distribution of households according to household per capita income. For health, the table shows the subsidy from NHS and SSS institutions, where SSS refers to the overall social security network including both Cajas Publicas and ICSS.

The total subsidy per household from education and health is remarkably constant across income groups. This constancy disappears, however, when subsidies are broken down by type of education and by type of health service. Subsidies for primary education are much larger for low-income households, and those for higher education are much smaller. NHS subsidies are higher for low-income families, whereas SSS subsidies are lower.

The constancy of the subsidy as expressed per household does not hold if expressed per capita, because household size is substantially larger in the poorest quintiles. The per capita subsidy for the richest quintile is 1.65 times the per capita subsidy for the poorest quintile.

Expressed as a percentage of the household income, the total subsidy is substantially larger for low-income groups: 24.5 percent of the household income for the poorest quintile, compared with 2.5 percent for the richest quintile.

Table 1.7. *Distribution of Income and Subsidies
for Education and Health, Classified by Income Quintiles*
(percentage)

Income quintile (poorest to richest)	Population	Income	Subsidies for education			
			Primary	Secondary	University	Average
1	25.1	5.2	32.1	16.8	0.8	19.8
2	22.7	9.1	26.7	21.8	4.6	20.2
3	19.4	12.6	20.5	21.2	10.7	18.6
4	17.4	18.7	14.5	24.6	23.5	20.1
5	15.4	54.4	6.2	15.6	60.4	21.3

Figure 1.2. *Distribution of Income and of Subsidies
for Health and Education, 1974*

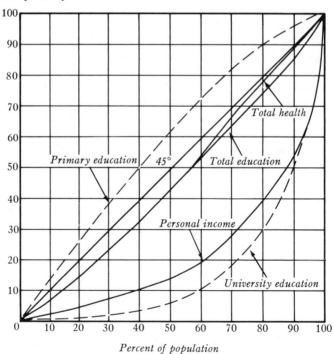

Percent of income/
Percent of subsidy

Percent of population

Subsidies for health			Average of subsidy for education and health
NHS	SSS	Average	
27.3	8.1	19.5	19.7
24.2	15.1	20.5	20.8
20.5	29.4	24.2	19.7
16.9	24.5	20.0	20.0
11.1	22.9	15.8	19.8

The distribution of the subsidies and the distribution of income are compared in Table 1.7 and Figure 1.2. Figure 1.2 represents a Lorenz relation: the population is ordered on the horizontal axis from lower to higher per capita income, and the accumulated distribution of income and subsidies corresponding to that population is shown on the vertical axis. The line for primary education lies above the diagonal: that is, lower-income groups have a larger share of the subsidy. The line for higher education not only lies below the diagonal, but actually below the line for the distribution of income: the distribution of the subsidy to higher education shows a stronger inequality than the distribution of personal income.

The lines for the total subsidy in education and health lie close together, between the diagonal and the line for the distribution of personal income. Thus, when mapped against the distribution of the population, the subsidy tends to favor higher-income groups, although it is more equally distributed than personal income.

Electricity, piped water, and sewerage

Data from the 1974 sample survey are also used to analyze the distribution of consumption and the availability of public utility services.

CONSUMPTION IN 1974 AND BETWEEN 1970 AND 1974. Table 1.8 shows, for the whole country, both the distribution of households

Table 1.8. *Households with Services in 1974*
and Households Which Were Connected to the Network
between 1970 and 1974, Classified by Income Groups
(percentage)

Income quintile (poorest to richest)	Electricity		Piped water		Sewerage		Street lighting	
	1974	1970–74	1974	1970–74	1974	1970–74	1974	1970–74
1	13.1	26.0	13.9	31.4	10.7	24.5	12.9	25.6
2	16.1	25.1	16.3	23.6	14.9	21.3	15.9	24.4
3	19.2	25.6	19.4	26.8	18.5	29.1	18.4	22.5
4	23.0	12.0	22.5	12.6	23.7	12.0	23.1	11.9
5	28.6	11.3	27.9	5.6	32.2	13.1	29.7	15.6
Urban	90.2	50.4	88.0	41.4	96.2	81.7	96.0	100.0

that reported having services in 1974 and that of households without services in 1970 but obtaining them between 1970 and 1974. The percentage of these households located in urban areas is also shown.

For 1974, the distribution of consumers by quintiles is similar across services: 25 to 30 percent of households with services belong to the poorest 40 percent of households, whereas 50 to 55 percent belong to the richest 40 percent. Almost all consumers live in urban areas.

Investment in electricity from all sources to generate and to transmit power fluctuated between 4.5 and 7.6 percent of the total government expenditure between 1970 and 1974, with the largest figure corresponding to 1974. For piped water and sewerage, these figures range between 1.7 and 2.7 percent. What income groups benefited from this investment?

To answer this question, households with the services in 1974 were asked whether they had had the services in 1970. With this information it is possible to compute the distribution of households that were connected to the service between 1970 and 1974. The data show that this distribution tends to benefit lower-income groups: 46 to 55 percent of the newly connected households belong to the poorest 40 percent of families. This is partly because investment has had a lower "urban bias." In the case of electricity and piped water, more than half of the newly connected house-holds are located in rural areas (as defined in this study).[10]

CONSUMPTION IN A SUPPLY-DEMAND CONTEXT. A multivariate analysis was made to identify variables associated with the con-sumption of services by households in urban areas. It was impor-tant to develop a framework in which this association could be interpreted to a certain extent as a cause-effect relation.

In this framework, a household comes under one of two classifi-cations: either it does not use a service because the supply network is geographically inaccessible, or it does not use the service be-cause—in spite of accessibility, that is, at the prices charged by the utility company—it has decided not to do so. The second situation is basically determined by demand.

Data from the sample survey show that households without services because of lack of demand represent a substantial per-centage of the households without services, particularly for elec-tricity and piped water. Thus, it is necessary to understand the reasons for this behavior to explain the different availability of services across households.

To do this, the factors influencing the probability of a household having a particular service, P, need to be identified. By using data on the individual characteristics of households with and without services, it is possible to estimate the influence of these charac-teristics on the probability of having the service.

The direct estimation of P does not fully capture the supply-demand mechanism discussed earlier. Hence, it does not allow the identification of the extent to which a particular variable or char-acteristic influences P through the demand or supply side. A more interesting specification of the problem is to think of P as the product of two probabilities to be estimated independently: the probability of a household being on the supply network of the service, P^s, that is, the probability of having access to the network at the connection cost institutionally set by public utility com-panies; and the probability of demanding the service, P^d, if offered at this connection cost. Both P^s and P^d are functions of a set of

10. Availability of piped water was defined as a situation in which the dwelling is connected to an aqueduct or to the primary water network. In rural areas, therefore, it includes households with any kind of access to a public aqueduct.

Table 1.9. *Electricity Use in Urban Areas:*
Estimates of the Linear Probability Function

Explanatory variables	Total urban			Poorest 40 percent[a]		
	P	P^d	P^s	P	P^d	P^s
1. Constant	0.75	0.79	0.88	0.77	0.75	1.00
	(13.89)	(15.12)	(24.25)	(5.0)	(5.21)	(9.80)
2. Intermediate cities	−0.04	−0.02	−0.02	−0.07	−0.05	−0.02
	(3.11)	(2.05)	(2.32)	(2.74)	(2.22)	(1.41)
3. Small towns	−0.14	−0.12	−0.03	−0.19	−0.17	−0.04
	(10.86)	(10.62)	(3.27)	(7.48)	(7.03)	(2.53)
4. Dirt floor	−0.36	−0.28	−0.15	−0.35	−0.27	−0.15
	(20.69)	(16.47)	(13.15)	(12.53)	(9.91)	(7.94)
5. Rural migrant	−0.11	−0.08	−0.04	−0.17	−0.16	−0.04
	(4.73)	(3.90)	(2.64)	(4.09)	(3.91)	(1.52)
6. Log of per capita income	0.02	0.02	0.002	−0.01	−0.01	0.004
	(2.28)	(2.64)	(0.39)	(0.22)	(0.22)	(0.13)
7. Log of years of schooling of head of household	0.08	0.06	0.03	0.17	0.13	0.05
	(5.21)	(4.17)	(2.91)	(4.70)	(3.95)	(2.17)
8. Log of age of head of household	0.09	0.07	0.06	0.11	0.14	−0.02
	(2.93)	(2.60)	(2.88)	(1.7)	(2.18)	(0.39)
Mean	0.92	0.94	0.97	0.84	0.88	0.95
R^2	0.31	0.24	0.12	0.30	0.24	0.11

Note: P = probability of a household having electricity; *P^s* = probability of a household being on the supply network for electricity; *P^d* = probability of a household demanding electricity. Figures in parentheses are *t* statistics.
a. Percentage of families according to household per capita income.
b. Not applicable.

variables to be estimated independently. The variables influencing *P^s* determine the utility company's behavior regarding the location of the network or supply; those influencing *P^d* are demand-oriented variables: that is, the cost of connection relative to the income of the household and other socioeconomic characteristics of households that govern such demand.

The actual estimation of *P*, *P^s*, and *P^d* was undertaken by defining a household on the supply network as one having a neighbor with the service within one block. This definition reasonably reflects a situation where a household can be connected if it is willing to pay a typical connection cost.

Poorest 20 percent[a]			Small towns		
P	P^d	P^s	P	P^d	P^s
0.67	0.68	0.95	0.30	0.10	0.62
(2.93)	(3.11)	(5.98)	(2.03)	(0.53)	(6.38)
−0.06	−0.05	−0.02	—b	—b	—b
(1.55)	(1.34)	(0.70)			
−0.20	−0.18	−0.04	—b	—b	—b
(5.16)	(4.89)	(1.48)			
−0.37	−0.28	−0.18	−0.46	−0.39	−0.18
(10.08)	(7.46)	(6.93)	(11.4)	(9.44)	(6.75)
−0.29	−0.28	−0.07	−0.19	−0.14	−0.99
(5.28)	(5.12)	(1.73)	(3.79)	(2.77)	(2.71)
−0.04	−0.04	0.01	0.08	0.11	0.005
(0.49)	(0.59)	(0.23)	(2.83)	(3.55)	(0.26)
0.18	0.17	0.03	0.18	0.16	0.06
(3.39)	(3.29)	(0.90)	(3.39)	(3.12)	(1.85)
0.22	0.23	0.01	0.18	0.28	0.20
(2.14)	(2.36)	(0.20)	(2.17)	(2.71)	(3.62)
0.81	0.86	0.94	0.76	0.81	0.93
0.35	0.28	0.13	0.31	0.26	0.14

Tables 1.9, 1.10, and 1.11 show the effects (coefficients) of different variables on P, P^s, and P^d. The results can be summarized as follows:

- The smaller the size of the city, the smaller the probability of having a service. This is particularly true for electricity and sewerage and is especially strong for the poorest quintile of urban households.
- When dirt floor, a characteristic of the dwelling, is introduced, the per capita income variable tends to become insignificant.[11] Dirt floor appears to be a more powerful demand variable in the case of electricity and piped water; the reverse is true for sewerage.

11. This was observed in experiments not reported here. The per capita income variable was always significant when dirt floor was not included.

Table 1.10. *Piped Water Use in Urban Areas:*
Estimates of the Linear Probability Function

Explanatory variables	Total urban			Poorest 40 percent[a]		
	P	P^d	P^s	P	P^d	P^s
1. Constant	0.84 (26.04)	0.92 (35.50)	0.91 (37.24)	0.73 (5.50)	0.91 (8.02)	0.76 (7.42)
2. Intermediate cities	−0.04 (2.97)	−0.02 (1.48)	−0.03 (2.57)	−0.04 (1.14)	−0.03 (0.99)	−0.01 (0.52)
3. Small towns	−0.06 (3.74)	−0.06 (4.53)	−0.004 (0.37)	−0.05 (1.79)	−0.07 (2.70)	−0.01 (0.46)
4. Dirt floor	−0.34 (16.34)	−0.23 (12.71)	−0.17 (10.95)	−0.33 (9.95)	−0.23 (7.67)	−0.17 (6.57)
5. Rural migrant	−0.07 (2.57)	−0.06 (2.74)	−0.01 (0.46)	−0.04 (0.77)	−0.05 (1.16)	0.02 (0.44)
6. Log of per capita income	0.04 (3.29)	0.02 (2.55)	0.02 (2.0)	0.07 (1.34)	0.03 (0.65)	0.06 (1.55)
7. Log of years of schooling of head of household	0.09 (4.96)	0.06 (3.83)	0.04 (2.70)	0.11 (2.57)	0.06 (1.61)	0.06 (1.79)
8. Log of years in same municipality	−0.03 (2.93)	−0.03 (3.48)	−0.002 (0.24)	−0.03 (1.58)	−0.03 (1.75)	−0.003 (0.17)
Mean	0.90	0.94	0.95	0.81	0.89	0.91
R^2	0.19	0.15	0.08	0.15	0.12	0.07

Note: P = probability of a household having piped water; P^s = probability of a household being on the supply network for piped water; P^d = probability of a household demanding piped water. Figures in parentheses are t statistics.
a. Percentage of families according to household per capita income.
b. Not applicable.

- The rural-migrant characteristic tends to operate on the demand side. It has a strong effect in the case of electricity for the poorest 40 percent of households.
- The log of years-of-schooling-of-head-of-household has a stronger effect in the poorer-income groups. A coefficient equal to 0.15 means that an increase of 50 percent in years of schooling will increase the probability by 7.5 percentage points.[12]

12. When the independent variable is defined in log form, the coefficient becomes $\Delta P / \Delta \log xi$.

Poorest 20 percent[a]			Small towns		
P	P^d	P^s	P	P^d	P^s
0.85	0.94	0.83	0.81	0.87	0.93
(4.09)	(5.21)	(5.01)	(9.81)	(11.64)	(15.97)
0.001	−0.01	0.01	—^{b}	—^{b}	—^{b}
(0.024)	(0.25)	(0.32)			
−0.03	−0.07	0.04	—^{b}	—^{b}	—^{b}
(0.59)	(1.75)	(1.12)			
−0.36	−0.23	−0.21	−0.33	−0.27	−0.12
(7.81)	(5.37)	(5.74)	(8.02)	(6.89)	(4.29)
−0.11	−0.11	0.01	−0.13	−0.12	−0.01
(1.57)	(1.93)	(0.16)	(2.49)	(2.50)	(0.37)
−0.01	0.003	0.02	0.05	0.05	0.01
(0.063)	(0.032)	(0.24)	(1.79)	(1.74)	(0.52)
0.14	0.10	0.04	0.09	0.05	0.04
(2.09)	(1.79)	(0.84)	(1.64)	(1.06)	(1.09)
−0.02	−0.03	0.01	−0.08	−0.06	−0.02
(0.55)	(0.96)	(0.59)	(3.38)	(3.11)	(1.09)
0.77	0.87	0.88	0.79	0.86	0.92
0.16	0.13	0.08	0.18	0.15	0.05

- The log of age-of-head-of-household was significant and was stronger on the demand side in the case of electricity. For the other services, it was not significant and was not included in the final regressions.
- A negative coefficient for the log of number-of-years-in-the-same-municipality for piped water and sewerage is not easy to interpret. It can be hypothesized that the longer the household remains without the service, the lower the probability that the household will have it today.

Given the nature of the sample, the data used in the analysis did not provide enough variation in the dependent variable. Most of the sampled households did have services, which reflects both the large coverage of services in urban Colombia and the fact that the design was geared more to obtaining statistically signifi-

Table 1.11. *Sewerage Use in Urban Areas:*
Estimates of the Linear Probability Function

Explanatory variables	Total urban			Poorest 40 percent[a]		
	P	P^d	P^s	P	P^d	P^s
1. Constant	0.79 (19.36)	0.92 (35.43)	0.86 (22.36)	0.57 (3.74)	0.73 (5.92)	0.77 (5.27)
2. Intermediate cities	−0.12 (6.78)	−0.02 (2.03)	−0.10 (6.29)	−0.13 (3.67)	−0.03 (0.99)	−0.12 (3.35)
3. Small towns	−0.15 (7.81)	−0.09 (6.81)	−0.09 (4.93)	−0.16 (4.49)	−0.12 (4.25)	−0.08 (2.45)
4. Dirt floor	−0.50 (18.87)	−0.21 (18.56)	−0.47 (18.81)	−0.43 (11.36)	−0.18 (4.49)	−0.43 (11.79)
5. Rural migrant	−0.06 (1.82)	−0.05 (2.22)	−0.02 (0.75)	−0.004 (0.07)	−0.01 (0.17)	−0.005 (0.09)
6. Log of per capita income	0.04 (3.10)	0.02 (2.46)	0.02 (1.76)	0.10 (1.64)	0.08 (1.55)	0.05 (0.85)
7. Log of years of schooling of head of household	0.16 (6.70)	0.05 (3.04)	0.13 (5.97)	0.22 (4.60)	0.12 (2.95)	0.17 (3.66)
8. Log of years in same municipality	−0.06 (4.90)	−0.02 (2.19)	−0.05 (4.24)	−0.06 (2.43)	−0.0002 (.014)	−0.07 (3.05)
Mean	0.80	0.95	0.84	0.66	0.90	0.73
R^2	0.27	0.11	0.23	0.24	0.10	0.21

Note: P = probability of a household having sewerage facilities; P^s = probability of a household being on the supply network for sewerage facilities; P^d = probability of a household demanding sewerage facilities. Figures in parentheses are t-statistics.
 a. Percentage of families according to household per capita income.
 b. Not applicable.

cant estimates for averages of the population than to hypothesis testing involving multivariate analysis (for the latter, an even stronger overrepresentation of low-income groups without services would have been required).

The relatively large number of households with services in the sample not only affects the overall variability of the dependent variable, but also influences the possibility of successfully separating supply and demand: that is, the factors behind P^d from

Poorest 20 percent[a]			Small towns		
P	P^d	P^s	P	P^d	P^s
0.85	0.73	1.08	0.58	0.67	0.80
(3.69)	(3.63)	(4.83)	(6.17)	(7.83)	(8.99)
−0.18	−0.06	−0.14	—b	—b	—b
(3.13)	(1.3)	(2.51)			
−0.20	−0.16	−0.11	—b	—b	—b
(3.89)	(3.52)	(2.17)			
−0.44	−0.22	−0.44	−0.47	−0.33	−0.44
(8.67)	(3.61)	(8.91)	(10.1)	(5.66)	(9.93)
0.01	−0.02	0.04	−0.06	−0.09	0.03
(0.19)	(0.31)	(0.53)	(0.99)	(1.84)	(0.46)
−0.04	0.07	−0.11	0.06	0.09	−0.01
(0.44)	(0.72)	(1.09)	(1.73)	(2.77)	(0.26)
0.22	0.13	0.18	0.26	0.10	0.24
(3.06)	(1.87)	(2.55)	(4.42)	(1.85)	(4.25)
−0.02	0.03	−0.05	−0.09	−0.03	−0.06
(0.69)	(1.07)	(1.64)	(3.32)	(1.37)	(2.51)
0.58	0.87	0.67	0.61	0.86	0.71
0.24	0.12	0.22	0.28	0.15	0.24

the factors behind P^s. Households with services not only have access to the supply network, they also demand services, and this prevents the necessary variation between the data used to estimate P^s and those used to estimate P^d.

Investment in roads and in agriculture

The sample survey attempted to measure the distribution of two large items of public expenditure in Colombia: investment in roads, which amounts to 4.3 percent of the total public expenditure, and investment in agriculture, which amounts to 4.0 percent.

Table 1.12. *Distribution of Subsidies and Beneficiaries*
of Government Services, 1974:
Results from the 1974 Sample Survey
(percentage)

| Income quintile (*poorest to richest*) | Distribution of the subsidy | | Households with service in 1974 and those who received it between 1970 and 1974 (Δ) | | | | | |
| | | | Electricity | | Piped water | | Sewerage | |
	Education	Health	1974	Δ	1974	Δ	1974	Δ
1	19.8	19.5	13.1	26.0	13.9	31.4	10.7	24.5
2	20.2	20.6	16.1	25.1	16.3	23.6	14.9	21.3
3	18.6	24.2	19.2	25.6	19.4	26.8	18.5	29.1
4	20.1	19.8	23.0	12.0	22.5	12.6	23.7	12.0
5	21.3	15.9	28.6	11.3	27.9	5.6	32.2	13.1
Urban	78.5[b]	77.3	90.2	50.4	88.0	41.4	96.2	81.7
As of percentage of government expenditure[e]	11.2	3.6	7.6[d]				2.5[d]	
GNP	2.2	0.7	1.5				0.5	

a. Not significantly different from zero.
b. Refers to the subsidy received by urban households from primary and secondary schools plus the subsidy to universities.
c. A figure of 62.7 billion pesos is used for government expenditure; see the text.
d. Refers to investment in 1974.
e. Refers to the grant component embodied in the new loans provided in 1974.
f. Equal to the running cost of SENA in 1974.

To capture the possible effect of public investment in roads, two variables were measured for both 1970 and 1974: the type of transportation used and the time of travel. They were derived from the following information: type of transportation of head of household to place of work; minutes it takes to walk from the dwelling to the nearest bus stop; for rural households, type of transportation to the urban conglomerate of the municipality; and time it takes to get to the urban conglomerate of the municipality.

No statistically significant change was observed in these variables between 1970 and 1974. Either investment in roads had an effect as an intermediate input (in the transportation of goods and services) instead of as a final service to be consumed directly

Households with service in 1974 and those							
who received it between 1970 and 1974 (Δ)				*Farm loans,*		*Educa-*	*Atten-*
Street		*Garbage*		*Caja Agraria*		*tional*	*dance at*
lighting		*collection*				*fellowships*	SENA
				(house-	*(Sub-*	*(house-*	*(man-*
1974	Δ	*1974*	Δ	*holds)*	*sidy)*[e]	*holds)*	*months)*
12.9	25.6	9.7	—[a]	34.6	19.6	16.2	11.3
15.9	24.4	12.9	—[a]	29.3	43.0	23.8	11.9
18.4	22.5	17.3	—[a]	19.5	20.2	9.7	24.3
23.1	11.9	24.1	—[a]	12.1	12.5	27.0	20.0
29.7	15.6	36.0	—[a]	4.5	4.7	23.3	32.5
96.0	100.0	100.0					100.0
					0.5		1.0[f]
					0.1		0.2

by households, or the technique used does not lend itself to measuring this type of public service.

Three variables related to farming activities were measured in rural areas: changes in the sources of irrigation water between 1970 and 1974; extension services received from public agencies during 1974; and new farming loans received from public agencies in 1974. The survey was unable to measure statistically significant values for the first two variables. It did, however, measure new farming loans received by households from the Caja Agraria, a public credit institution.

Other services

Other services measured were garbage collection in urban areas; educational fellowships from public sources; and attendance at the Servicio Nacional de Aprendizaje (SENA), the major adult retraining institution. The distribution of these services by income groups is presented in Table 1.12.

Services studied in relation to total government expenditure

The results presented earlier are summarized in Table 1.12. The expenditure in the services studied accounts for 26.4 percent of total government expenditure (62.7 thousand million pesos) and 5.2 percent of Colombia's GNP in 1974 (323 thousand million pesos).[13] If the service of the debt is excluded from the definition of public expenditures, the above fraction increases to 33.2 percent of total public spending. The largest subsidy is to the educational sector and accounts for 11.2 percent of government expenditure. Of this total, 4.7 corresponds to primary, 4.1 to secondary, and 2.4 to higher education.

Appendix. Socioeconomic Stratification of Large Cities

In 1970 the Colombian Bureau of Census (DANE) carried out a stratification of the neighborhoods of the four largest cities—Bogotá, Cali, Medellín, and Barranquilla—by socioeconomic indicators. The indicators obtained from the 1970 household survey and from the agencies in charge of urbanization in each city are: average per capita income of the neighborhood; construction materials of the house; availability of public services and durable goods; index of crowding; and average educational level.

13. The figures for public expenditures are derived as follows:

Consolidated Fiscal Budget for 1974 (million pesos)

Current	45.500
Investment	34.014
Total	79.514
Minus: Income public companies	−16.836
Total	62.678
Minus: Service public debt	−12.987
Total	49.691

Source: Contraloría General de la República de Colombia, *Informe Financiero de 1974* (processed) pp. 818, 819, 821.

The relation between the six strata used by DANE and the four strata used in the 1974 sample survey is:

1974 sample survey	DANE *(1970)*
1. Slums	1. Lowest income
2. Low income	2. Low income
	3. Low middle
3. Middle	4. Middle
4. High	5. High middle
	6. High

Chapter 2

The Distribution of Income
and Other Poverty Indicators

NEW ESTIMATES OF the distribution of income in Colombia have been made based on the data collected in the 1974 sample survey. Other socioeconomic characteristics of households, which indicate the level of welfare, are reported also.

Distribution of Income

The 1974 survey recorded data on household income for the month before the interview. Because less than ten minutes of each interview was spent in deriving the income data, they may be less reliable than those usually obtained from budget and consumption surveys in which more time is given to obtaining this variable. The monthly household income figure was obtained by identifying the income earners in the family and by computing the sources of income for each. On the questionnaire five sources of income were defined: labor and wage income; income in kind received from the employer; value of the food grown and consumed on the site or plot; net profits from business or farm operations; and pension payments.

The 1974 sample survey

Urban, rural, and countrywide income distribution data were presented in Table 1.3, above. The data suggest that rural income is more evenly distributed than urban, particularly at the lower

Figure 2.1. *Distribution of Income, 1974:*
Rural and Urban Differences

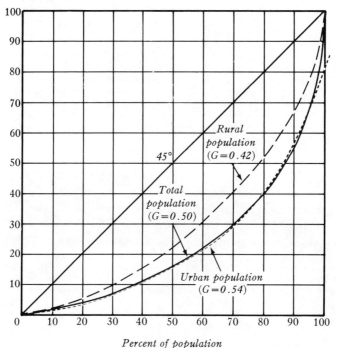

Percent of income

Percent of population

levels. The poorest 20 percent of families in urban areas receive only 4.6 percent of the total urban income, whereas the poorest 20 percent of rural households receive 7.6 percent of the total rural income. These results still hold if the distribution of population rather than households is considered. This is illustrated in Figure 2.1, where the accumulated percentage of the population, ordered according to per capita income, is plotted against the accumulated income. The Gini coefficient is 0.54 for urban areas, 0.42 for rural areas, and 0.50 for the country as a whole.

The effect of differences in rural and urban incomes is shown in Table 2.1, which classifies households in each quintile of the country income distribution according to their location. Rural households represent 53.4 percent of those in the lowest-income

Table 2.1. *Percentage of Families in Each Income Quintile, Classified by Location*

Income quintile (poorest to richest)	Large cities	Inter-mediate cities	Small towns	Urban total	Rural areas
1	13.0	10.8	22.8	46.6	53.4
2	18.2	13.5	18.6	50.3	49.7
3	25.5	16.1	14.5	56.1	43.9
4	34.1	22.5	13.1	69.7	30.3
5	54.2	24.7	8.3	87.2	12.8
Total	28.9	17.5	15.5	61.9	38.1

Note: Percentages add to 100 across rows.

quintile and only 12.8 percent of those in the highest, whereas households in large cities represent only 13 percent of those in the lowest-income quintile but 54.2 percent of those in the highest.[1]

In Chapter 1 it was shown how income data can also be used to compute the fraction of the population receiving a per capita income lower than a predetermined value such as a poverty line. Table 1.4 showed that the percentage of families in each region below commonly used poverty lines is highly sensitive to the exchange rate used.

Comparison with other studies

Income distribution estimates are difficult to compare.[2] Studies differ in the definition of income, reliability of measurement, representativeness, and type of population unit used. When the household is the unit of measurement, the distribution of households or population according to household per capita income is usually derived; when the individual in the labor force is the unit of measurement, the distribution usually refers to active population or to income recipients.

1. A proper comparison obviously requires an adjustment for differences in the purchasing power of urban and rural nominal incomes. To the extent that this purchasing power is greater in rural areas, these figures exaggerate the percentage of the rural population in the poorest quintile of the total population.

2. See Shail Jain, *Size Distribution of Income: A Compilation of Data* (Baltimore: Johns Hopkins University Press for the World Bank, 1975).

Perhaps the most comprehensive and reliable estimate of income distribution in Colombia is that of Berry and Urrutia (B-U).[3] Their study is concerned with the economically active population and uses a variety of sources of data. The estimate of income distribution for the country combines an urban estimate based on unemployment surveys made between 1967 and 1969 by the Centro de Estudios del Desarrollo Económico, Universidad de Los Andes (CEDE) and an estimate for rural areas based on the 1960 agricultural census and the 1964 population census.[4]

Table 2.2 presents a comparison of Berry and Urrutia's estimates and those arrived at in this study. Lorenz curves and Gini coefficients for total country estimates were shown in Figure 1.1.

Comparisons between the income distribution of households or population and that of the active population (B-U) must take into account the differences across income groups in the number of earners per household as well as in the number of dependents per earner. If low-income groups have a lower number of earners per household, the distribution of households will show a greater inequality than the distribution of the active population. If there are a larger number of dependents per earner in low-income groups, the distribution of the total population will show a greater inequality than the distribution of the active population.

If poorer families have larger family size, a lower number of income earners per household means a larger number of dependents per earner. Consequently, if the distribution of households shows a greater inequality than the distribution of the active population, the same will be true for the distribution of the total population. The data in Table 2.2 and Figure 1.1 show different results. The distributions for households and individuals in the 1974 sample survey show greater equality than the B-U estimates for the active population, particularly in the rural area.

Gini coefficients

The marked difference for the rural area (for B-U, the Gini coefficient is 0.57; for the sample survey, it is 0.42) is largely ex-

---

3. Albert Berry and Miguel Urrutia, *Income Distribution in Colombia* (New Haven: Yale University Press, 1976).

4. Ibid., p. 28.

Table 2.2. *Income Distribution Comparison*
(percentage)

	Urban					Rural		
	1974 sample survey			*1964 Berry-Urrutia*		*1974 sample survey*		
House-holds	*Popula-tion*	*Income*	*Active popula-tion*	*Income*	*House-holds*	*Popula-tion*	*Income*
10	12.5	1.7	12.7	0.6	10	13.4	3.0
20	24.7	4.6	25.0	2.5	20	24.9	7.6
30	36.7	8.6	30.3	4.5	30	36.6	13.8
40	46.9	13.3	41.0	9.8	40	47.7	20.9
50	56.8	18.9	51.1	15.7	50	59.2	29.8
60	66.1	25.5	60.0	21.7	60	68.6	38.6
70	75.5	34.2	70.2	30.2	70	76.7	47.5
80	84.4	45.7	79.3	40.1	80	85.5	59.4
90	92.6	62.3	89.8	56.3	90	93.5	73.5
95	98.5	73.9	96.0	72.9	95	97.0	81.9

plained by the different estimates of income for the upper 5 percent of households. In Berry and Urrutia's study, 5.1 percent of the richest active population received 40.4 percent of the rural income; in the 1974 sample survey, the richest 5 percent of households received 18.1 percent of the rural income. Berry and Urrutia in-

Table 2.3. *Comparison of Gini Coefficients from Four Studies*

Year	Study	Urban	Rural	Country
1964	Berry-Urrutia (economically active population)	0.55	0.57	0.57
1967	Rafael Prieto (households in four largest cities)	0.47	—a	—a
1970	DANE–Polibio Córdoba (income recipients)	0.55	—a	—a
1974	1974 sample survey			
	Population	0.54	0.42	0.50
	Households	0.48	0.32	0.47

a. Data reported only for urban category.
Source: All figures, except those for the 1974 sample survey, were taken from Berry and Urrutia, *Income Distribution in Colombia*, Chapter 2.

Rural		Total country				
1964 Berry-Urrutia		*1974 sample survey*			*1964 Berry-Urrutia*	
Active population	*Income*	*House-holds*	*Population*	*Income*	*Active population*	*Income*
11.1	1.8	10	13.0	1.9	8.8	0.54
18.7	4.1	20	25.1	5.2	25.1	4.0
30.1	8.5	30	36.5	9.4	—	—
36.8	10.8	40	47.2	14.3	42.2	9.6
50.0	16.6	50	57.7	20.4	52.5	14.5
61.5	22.7	60	66.9	26.9	60.9	19.6
73.4	30.4	70	75.7	34.9	72.1	28.6
80.5	36.5	80	84.4	45.6	80.0	36.9
90.2	49.4	90	92.5	60.7	89.1	50.6
94.9	59.6	95	96.4	72.8	95.6	66.3

clude in the rural distribution high-income landowners living in cities, whereas the 1974 sample does not; in this respect, the two estimates are not directly comparable.

Table 2.3 gives Gini coefficient estimates from the B-U study as well as two others—DANE-Polibio Córdoba (1970) and Prieto (1967)—and allows comparison with estimates from the 1974 sample survey for the distribution of population and households, both ranked according to per capita household income. The smaller coefficient for households in the sample reflects the strong negative association between per capita income and family size, particularly in rural areas. The coefficient for urban areas is practically the same whether the economically active population (B-U), income recipients (DANE-Polibio Córdoba), or the total population (1974 sample survey) is used. For the country total, the 1974 survey estimate appears lower (0.50) than the B-U estimate (0.57).

Other Poverty Indicators

The 1974 sample survey collected data on other variables that can be considered poverty indicators. Table 2.4 presents the dis-

Table 2.4. *Distribution of Heads of Household in Each Quintile, by Years of Schooling*
(percentage of total in quintile)

Income quintile (poorest to richest)	Years of schooling				
	0	1	2	3	4
1	31.4	6.7	20.6	15.0	8.6
2	27.7	6.3	18.9	16.3	9.8
3	22.7	4.1	17.3	15.4	8.6
4	19.2	3.2	9.7	10.5	8.6
5	8.6	1.5	5.4	4.3	5.4
Country average	22.0	4.4	14.4	12.2	8.2

Note: Percentages add to 100 across rows.

tribution of heads of households in each quintile according to years of schooling completed. The last row shows the distribution for the total country. More than a fifth of the total heads of household have no schooling, perhaps the best indicator of illiteracy. As expected, the amount of schooling is strongly associated with the income level of the head of household: 31.4 percent in the poorest quintile have no schooling, whereas this is true of only 8.6 percent in the richest. In the two poorest quintiles, almost no heads of household have completed secondary school (11 years). Only in the richest quintile have any heads of household completed the university (16 years).

Data on means and standard deviations for other socioeconomic indicators, classified by location and income quintile, are presented in the statistical appendix, Tables SA-3 to SA-17. Information on sample size and some statistical formulas for identifying significance of test of the difference of two means are given in the appendix to this chapter. Table 2.5 presents means and standard deviation for some of these indicators, classified by quintiles in the distribution of income. The data tend to show that the number of dependents per earner (the ratio of column 1 over column 2) varies sharply across income groups, being substantially larger for low-income households. This result, however, is highly sensitive to the definition of the "number of earners" variable, particularly in an environment where second earners seldom receive monetary incomes. A comparison between columns 1 and 3 suggests that

	Years of schooling			
5 (primary)	6–10	11 (secondary)	12–15	16 (university)
12.8	4.2	0.3	0.4	0
14.3	5.9	0.2	0.6	0
18.1	11.5	1.2	1.1	0
22.7	18.5	3.8	3.3	0.5
15.2	23.6	15.5	9.2	11.3
16.6	12.8	4.2	2.8	2.4

number of persons per room is substantially higher for the lowest-income groups. The availability of toilets or latrines has an even stronger positive association with income.

The occupational characteristics of the heads of household in the poorest quintile should be an important consideration for policy

Table 2.5. *Mean and Standard Deviations of Socioeconomic Variables of Households*

Income quintile (poorest to richest)	Mean number of					
	Persons in household	Income earners in household	Rooms occupied by household	Toilets or latrines in dwelling	Years of schooling of head of household	Years of schooling of wife
1	6.87 (2.5)	1.24 (0.8)	2.51 (1.3)	0.59 (0.6)	2.29 (2.2)	1.67 (1.9)
2	5.99 (2.5)	1.37 (0.9)	2.58 (1.3)	0.70 (0.7)	2.60 (2.4)	1.93 (2.1)
3	5.38 (2.5)	1.52 (1.0)	2.74 (1.5)	0.86 (0.7)	3.22 (2.7)	2.47 (2.8)
4	4.80 (2.4)	1.59 (1.0)	3.13 (1.7)	1.01 (0.8)	4.36 (3.5)	3.22 (3.4)
5	4.25 (2.3)	1.72 (1.0)	4.40 (2.3)	1.81 (1.2)	7.84 (4.8)	5.34 (5.0)
Country average	5.47 (2.6)	1.48 (0.9)	3.07 (1.8)	0.99 (0.9)	4.05 (3.8)	2.91 (3.5)

Note: Standard deviations are given in parentheses.

Table 2.6. *Distribution of Heads of Household in the Poorest Income Quintile According to Location, Sector, and Occupation*

Location and occupation	Percentage of heads of household	
Urban areas		
Self-employed		
a. Manufacturing	5.2	16.0
b. Services	10.8	
Wage labor		
a. Manufacturing	4.9	
b. Construction	5.5	18.6
c. Services	8.2	
Rural areas		
a. Landowners		25.6
b. Sharecroppers	6.6	
c. Tenants and tenant farmers	3.9	18.6
d. Agricultural labor living on farms	8.1	
e. Households not living on farms		14.0
Ill-defined occupations		7.2

intervention. Table 2.6 presents the percentage distribution of heads of household in the poorest quintile, classified by location, sector, and occupation. The results are tentative, since the questionnaire did not allow for a precise definition of borderline occupations, which are common in poor income groups. For example, a large fraction of those with ill-defined occupations (7.2 percent) were self-employed heads of household working at home.

A similar problem arose in classifying occupations in the rural area. All rural heads of household classified in Table 2.6 under (a), (b), (c), and (d) live on farms and participate directly in farming activities; (d) was calculated residually, and it is not clear whether it can be interpreted as pure wage labor or farm labor. Similarly, although heads of household in (e) do not live on farms (rural areas include towns of less than 1,500 inhabitants), they may be directly involved in farming activities.

Most heads of household in the poverty group live in the rural area, around 60 percent, depending on whether those with ill-defined occupations are included. The highest fraction—25 percent—is made up of landowners, that is, small farmers. Nonland-owners living on farms and directly involved in farming activities represent 18.6 percent. In rural areas, heads of household not living on farms represent 14.0 percent. In urban areas, heads of household are evenly classified between wage labor (mostly in the service sector) and self-employment. This implies that policies aimed at increasing the earning capacity of the poorest 20 percent of households will require several different points of intervention.

Appendix. Socioeconomic Characteristics of Households

Data derived from the 1974 sample survey on means and standard deviations of socioeconomic variables of households are presented in the statistical appendix, Tables SA-3 to SA-17. The data are classified by quintiles in the income distribution (or household per capita income) of each respective location or area: small towns, intermediate cities, large cities, urban average, rural areas, and country average. This appendix presents sample size and formulas to interpret the statistical significance of the difference between these means.

Sample size

Table 2.7 shows the sample size corresponding to each (expanded) quintile. For a given location, the sample size differs across quintiles, because the mean expansion factor of each quintile differs, particularly for the large cities. This situation results from the fact that the low-income neighborhoods in large cities purposely were overrepresented in the survey. For the same reason, the sum of locational sample sizes for a given quintile does not necessarily add up to the aggregate sample sizes of each quintile.

Statistical significance of the test of the difference of two means

Table 2.8 indicates the degree of statistical significance of the differences of two means. When the variance of the two populations (σ_1 and σ_2) are unknown and presumed unequal and when samples

Table 2.7. *Sample Size in Each (Expanded) Quintile*

Income quintile (poorest to richest)	Number of households					
	Large cities	Inter-mediate cities	Small towns	Urban total	Rural areas	Country total
1	285	208	137	663	278	863
2	259	227	155	624	261	886
3	209	188	145	567	239	796
4	152	198	150	499	252	786
5	145	173	138	416	220	688
Total	1,050	994	725	2,769	1,250	4,019

Note: The quintiles are determined according to the expanded distribution of household per capita income in each region. The urban and country totals for a given income quintile are not necessarily arithmetic totals of the locational sample sizes because, for large cities, low-income neighborhoods were purposely overrepresented in the survey.

Table 2.8. *Critical Values of d_{Min} (5 Percent Significance Level) for the Test of Means under Alternative Combinations of Sample Sizes*

		N_1						
		800	700	500	300	250	200	150
	800	0.08						
	700	0.09	0.09					
	500	0.10	0.10	0.11				
N_2	300			0.12	0.14			
	250				0.15	0.15		
	200				0.16	0.16	0.17	
	150				0.17	0.18	0.19	0.20

are large, the test of means becomes:

$$t = \frac{\bar{X}_1 - \bar{X}_2}{\sqrt{(S_1^2/N_1) + (S_2^2/N_2)}},$$

where $\bar{X}_i$ are the sample means, S_i^2 the variance of the samples, and N_i the respective sample size. t has a "Student" distribution, but it can be referred to a table of normal probabilities for large sample sizes.

The subscript 1 will be used for the sample with the larger standard deviation of the two being compared:

$$S_2 = a\, S_1, \qquad \text{where } a \leq 1$$

$$S_2{}^2 = a^2 S_1{}^2.$$

Substituting into t, the result is:

$$t = \frac{(\bar{X}_1 - \bar{X}_2)}{S_1 \sqrt{(1/N_1) + (a^2/N_2)}} \,.$$

Denoting $d_{Min} = (\bar{X}_1 - \bar{X}_2)/S_1$ as the difference of the means expressed as a fraction of the largest standard deviation (which correspondingly becomes the minimum or lowest of the two possible ratios) generates:

$$t \sqrt{(1/N_1) + (a^2/N_2)} = d_{Min}.$$

At a 5 percent significance level, rejection of the null hypothesis that the means come from the same population implies (for a positive $X_1 - X_2$):

$$1.645 \sqrt{(1/N_1) + (a^2/N_2)} = \leq d_{Min}.$$

Table 2.8 presents those critical values of d_{Min} by assuming that $a^2 = 1$: that is, both standard deviations are equal. If a^2 is less than 1, the critical values of d_{Min} will represent a stronger test than the one required.

Chapter 3

The Distribution
of Public Subsidies for Education

To ESTIMATE THE EDUCATION SUBSIDIES received by different income groups in the population, two sets of data are required: enrollment in each type of education from each income group and the subsidy per student year for each type of education.

The first part of this chapter presents data derived from the 1974 sample survey on enrollment by income groups. The second presents data on public subsidies to the educational sector, prepared especially for this study by the Compañía Colombiana de Datos (COLDATOS). The estimates of the preceding sections are then combined, and the distribution of subsidies across income groups are derived.

Enrollment by Income Group

Table 3.1 classifies students enrolled in each type of education according to quintiles in the country distribution of income. Because approximately 97 percent of the total subsidy for education goes to public education, the enrollment in public schools in each income group becomes the most important determinant of the distributive content of this subsidy. Table 3.1 shows that low-income quintiles have a larger share of enrollment in primary public schools, whereas the opposite is true in higher public education. Of the children enrolled in public primary education, 32.1 percent belong to the poorest quintile, whereas only 5.8 percent come from the richest. In higher public education 5.8 percent of

Table 3.1. *School Enrollment, Classified by Income Group, 1974*
(percentage)

Income quintile (poorest to richest)	Primary schools			Secondary schools			Universities		
	Pub-lic	Pri-vate	Aver-age	Pub-lic	Pri-vate	Aver-age	Pub-lic	Pri-vate	Aver-age
1	32.1	11.9	*28.6*	16.7	9.8	*13.4*	0.9	0	*0.5*
2	27.9	13.8	*25.5*	23.0	9.8	*16.7*	4.9	2.3	*3.8*
3	20.0	19.3	*19.9*	21.1	14.5	*17.9*	10.9	4.7	*8.1*
4	14.2	19.8	*15.2*	24.9	22.5	*23.8*	23.8	16.5	*20.4*
5	5.8	35.2	*10.8*	14.3	43.4	*28.2*	59.5	76.5	*67.2*

the students come from the poorest 40 percent of households, whereas 59.5 percent come from the richest quintile.

The sharp skewness observed for primary and higher education does not hold for secondary public education. Enrollment by income group shows less variation and tends to favor the middle-income quintiles.

Estimating the amount of subsidy received by each household requires information on the number of students per household and on the levels and types of schooling they attend. The 1974 sample survey provides these data for public schools, for private schools that received subsidies in 1974, and for private schools without subsidies. The data on enrollment from each household were adjusted by whatever discrepancy was found between the aggregate enrollment figures from the expanded sample survey and the figures reported by the Ministry of Education. Table 3.2 compares these aggregate figures and provides the corresponding adjustment factor; except in public higher education, this factor is not significant. The adjusted enrollment data are shown in Table 3.3.

Tables 3.4 and 3.5 present the adjusted figures on enrollment per household. To allow, the discussion of the factors determining variations in enrollment, data on the number of children in each household are given in Table 3.6.

Primary schools

Table 3.4 shows again the large difference across income groups in the enrollment per household in public primary schools. On

Table 3.2. *School Enrollment: Comparison between Sample Survey Figures and Ministry of Education Figures, 1974*
(thousands of students)

| | Primary schools | | | | | |
| | Public | | | Private | | |
	Urban	Rural	Total	Urban	Rural	Total
Sample survey	1,698	1,195	2,893	565	31	596
Ministry of Education	1,919	1,188	3,107	528	32	560
Adjustment ratio	1.13	0.99	1.07	0.93	1.03	0.93

Source: Ministerio de Educación, (processed). ICFES, "La Educación en Cifras, 1970–74." The figures exclude "territorios nacionales."

the average, households belonging to the poorest income quintile have 1.38 children enrolled in public primary schools, whereas the ones in the richest quintile have only 0.26. This is mainly because richer families have less children of school age (see Table 3.6) and because they tend to send their children to private schools, especially if they live in the urban areas. In the urban areas, families belonging to the richest quintile have 0.31 children in private primary schools, whereas only 0.26 are enrolled in public primary schools.

Except for the highest income group, enrollment per household in public primary schools is larger in urban areas, even though these households also have a large enrollment in private schools. The basic reason for this is the larger overall enrollment rate in urban areas.

Secondary schools

There is a great difference in the enrollment per household in public secondary education between urban and rural areas, particularly in low-income groups. Rural households in the poorest 40 percent of households have only 0.07 students enrolled in public schools and none in private schools. The difference appears even more significant when the comparison is made for the total en-

Secondary schools						Universities		
Public			Private			Public	Private	Total
Urban	Rural	Total	Urban	Rural	Total			
588	133	*721*	629	37	*666*	90	74	*164*
0	0	*641*	0	0	*624*	73	76	*149*
0	0	*0.89*	0	0	*0.94*	0.81	1.02	*0.91*

rollment (in all schools) per household, which is four to five times larger for urban households.

Enrollment per household in public secondary schools tends to be highest for the second, third, and fourth quintiles: that is, for the middle classes. The reasons for a lower enrollment in the

Table 3.3 *Adjusted School Enrollment, Classified by Location of Households, 1974*
(thousands of students)

Location	Primary schools			Secondary schools			Universities[a]	
		Private			Private			
	Public	With subsidies	Without subsidies	Public	With subsidies	Without subsidies	Public	Private
Large cities	746	73	219	192	90	268	—	—
Intermediate cities	556	41	134	181	51	111	—	—
Small towns	617	13	48	150	35	42	—	—
Urban total	1,919	127	401	523	176	421	—	—
Rural area	1,188	5	27	118	0	27	—	—
Country total	3,107	132	428	641	176	448	73	76

a. Results for universities are only given as country totals since the data were not broken down by location.

Table 3.4. *Mean Enrollment per Household in Different Types of Primary Schools, Classified by Quintiles*
(number of students)

Income quintile (poorest to richest)	Large cities				Intermediate cities				Small towns			
	T_1	T_2	T_3	Total	T_1	T_2	T_3	Total	T_1	T_2	T_3	Total
1	1.49	0.07	0.07	1.63	1.68	0.05	0.19	1.92	1.37	0	0.15	1.52
2	1.30	0.10	0.17	1.57	1.34	0.06	0.20	1.60	1.43	0	0.06	1.40
3	0.79	0.08	0.26	1.13	1.14	0.05	0.20	1.39	1.24	0.06	0.05	1.35
4	0.78	0.06	0.18	1.02	0.70	0.06	0.20	0.96	0.61	0.03	0.02	0.66
5	0.25	0.06	0.25	0.56	0.26	0.09	0.25	0.60	0.34	0.05	0.14	0.53
Country average	0.71	0.07	0.20	0.98	0.88	0.07	0.21	1.16	1.10	0.02	0.08	1.20

Note: T_1 = public schools; T_2 = private schools with subsidies; T_3 = private schools without subsidies.

Table 3.5. *Mean Enrollment per Household in Different Types of Secondary Schools, Classified by Quintiles*
(number of students)

Income quintile (poorest to richest)	Large cities				Intermediate cities				Small towns			
	T_1	T_2	T_3	Total	T_1	T_2	T_3	Total	T_1	T_2	T_3	Total
1	0.19	0.10	0.13	0.42	0.30	0.05	0.08	0.43	0.24	0.09	0.09	0.42
2	0.31	0.04	0.15	0.50	0.41	0.07	0.08	0.56	0.28	0.09	0.05	0.42
3	0.28	0.01	0.15	0.50	0.28	0.08	0.16	0.52	0.20	0.09	0.12	0.41
4	0.20	0.08	0.25	0.53	0.32	0.07	0.17	0.56	0.33	0.05	0.07	0.45
5	0.08	0.11	0.37	0.56	0.18	0.12	0.28	0.58	0.36	0.05	0.19	0.60
Country average	0.18	0.09	0.25	0.52	0.29	0.08	0.27	0.54	0.27	0.06	0.08	0.43

Note: T_1 = public schools; T_2 = private schools with subsidies; T_3 = private schools without subsidies.

richest and poorest quintiles can be understood by comparing Tables 3.5 and 3.6. In the poorest quintile, the low enrollment in public schools reflects the extremely low total school enrollment relative to the number of children ages 13 to 19. Of the 1.40 children per household between 13 and 19 years old, there are 0.24 children enrolled—a rate of 17 percent. In the richest quintile, although the total enrollment rate is much higher (on the order of 62 percent or 0.50 children out of 0.80 between 13 and 19 years

Urban average				Rural areas				Country average			
T_1	T_2	T_3	Total	T_1	T_2	T_3	Total	T_1	T_2	T_3	Total
1.48	0.04	0.16	*1.68*	1.26	0	0.02	*1.28*	1.38	0.02	0.08	*1.48*
1.33	0.05	0.13	*1.51*	0.98	0	0.01	*0.99*	1.15	0.03	0.08	*1.26*
1.00	0.06	0.19	*1.25*	0.72	0.01	0.02	*0.75*	0.88	0.04	0.11	*1.03*
0.72	0.05	0.15	*0.92*	0.41	0	0.03	*0.44*	0.62	0.04	0.11	*0.77*
0.26	0.07	0.24	*0.57*	0.27	0	0.03	*0.30*	0.26	0.06	0.21	*0.53*
0.86	0.06	0.18	*1.10*	0.86	0	0.02	*0.88*	0.86	0.04	0.12	*1.02*

Urban average				Rural areas				Country average			
T_1	T_2	T_3	Total	T_1	T_2	T_3	Total	T_1	T_2	T_3	Total
0.24	0.09	0.10	*0.43*	0.07	0	0.02	*0.09*	0.15	0.04	0.05	*0.24*
0.33	0.05	0.09	*0.47*	0.07	0	0.03	*0.10*	0.20	0.02	0.06	*0.28*
0.26	0.08	0.14	*0.48*	0.10	0	0.01	*0.11*	0.19	0.04	0.08	*0.31*
0.27	0.07	0.19	*0.53*	0.12	0	0.02	*0.14*	0.22	0.05	0.15	*0.42*
0.13	0.11	0.33	*0.57*	0.09	0	0.02	*0.11*	0.13	0.09	0.28	*0.50*
0.23	0.08	0.19	*0.50*	0.09	0	0.02	*0.12*	0.18	0.05	0.12	*0.35*

old), enrollment in public schools is only about a third of that in private schools, 0.13 and 0.37, respectively.

Universities

Enrollment per household in universities, which is highly correlated with the level of household per capita income, is shown in Table 3.7. For the middle-income quintiles enrollment per household in public universities is approximately twice as high as in

Table 3.6. *Number of Children per Household,*
Classified by Location, Age, and Income Quintile

Income quintile (poorest to richest)	Large cities			Intermediate cities		
	All ages	6–12	13–19	All ages	6–12	13–19
1	6.33	1.83	1.35	6.83	1.87	1.41
2	6.11	1.61	1.34	6.09	1.40	1.46
3	5.36	1.21	1.04	5.98	1.45	1.24
4	5.12	0.96	1.04	4.96	0.91	1.00
5	4.38	0.63	0.81	4.40	0.68	0.82
Country average	5.12	1.05	1.03	5.40	1.13	1.12

Table 3.7. *Mean Enrollment per Household in Universities,*
Classified by Quintiles
(number of students)

Income quintile (poorest to richest)	Public	Private	Total
1	0.001	0	0.001
2	0.005	0.002	0.007
3	0.011	0.005	0.016
4	0.024	0.017	0.042
5	0.061	0.081	0.142
Country average	0.020	0.021	0.041

private universities. The reverse is true for the richest quintile, where household enrollment is 0.061 in public universities and 0.081 in private universities.

Public Subsidy per Student Year

The concept of subsidy as it is used here includes all public contributions—whether from the central government, department,

Small towns			Rural areas			Country average		
All ages	*6–12*	*13–19*	*All ages*	*6–12*	*13–19*	*All ages*	*6–12*	*13–19*
6.93	2.02	1.44	6.99	2.14	1.42	6.87	2.05	1.40
5.93	1.52	1.21	5.95	1.47	1.24	5.99	1.50	1.28
5.60	1.27	1.20	5.12	1.05	1.06	5.38	1.19	1.10
4.53	0.57	1.00	4.41	0.68	0.81	4.80	0.81	0.96
4.32	0.59	0.90	3.39	0.35	0.60	4.25	0.59	0.80
5.76	1.37	1.20	5.63	1.37	1.14	5.50	1.23	1.11

or city—to the yearly operating cost of schools.[1] For public schools the subsidy is basically equal to the labor cost (teachers' salaries). The estimate does not include the opportunity cost of the stock of physical capital invested in education: that is, depreciation and interest on public buildings.

To compute the subsidy per student, the 1974 sample survey classification for schools was used: public schools, where practically all operating costs are financed out of public funds, and private schools, which receive some public funding.

Public primary schools

To capture not only urban-rural differences but also intraurban and intrarural variations, the subsidy was broken down into the forty-eight geographic strata of the sample survey. This dictated the choice of both method and data used to derive the subsidy per student year.

The operating cost of public primary schools is financed by the central government and by the department and municipality where each school is located. The institutional mechanism through

1. Estimates given in this chapter are based on the COLDATOS report. Compañía Colombiana de Datos (COLDATOS), "Unit Cost of Education and Health Services in Colombia in 1974" ("Costos Unitarios de los Servicios de Educación y Salud en Colombia en 1974") (study prepared for the World Bank, Bogotá, 1976; processed).

which these funds are allocated to specific schools is the Regional Educational Fund (FER). The Instituto Colombiano de Pedagogia (ICOLPE) has reported data for 1973 on the budgeted contributions from all sources for each of the twenty-three departments in the country.[2] Actual expenditure for that year was derived on the basis of the historical evolution of budgeted and actual contributions over the previous six years. The coefficient of proportionality for each department was estimated through regression analysis and was applied to the budgeted figure for 1973 (Table 3.8).

The next step was to break down the contribution by department to figures for each of the forty-eight regional strata used in the sample survey. In 1972 the Bureau of Census (DANE) surveyed a sample of 17,000 schools to gather information on the number of teachers and their classification according to four wage categories.[3] With these data it was possible to derive the distribution of teachers in each stratum according to wage categories.

By applying this percentage distribution to the total by department,[4] it was possible to arrive at the number of teachers in each wage category employed in each stratum. This information, together with data on teachers' wages, provides an estimate of the total cost of teachers for each stratum.[5,6] The difference between the cost of teachers for each department and the total public contribution was distributed across the different strata in proportion to the number of students in each stratum.

Table 3.9 shows the total public contribution for each stratum as estimated for 1973 and the number of students and subsidy per student for 1973. The subsidy per student for 1974 was obtained by multiplying the 1973 figure by 1.20 to allow for the 20 percent average increase in teachers' salaries between these years.

Public secondary schools

The subsidy per student in public secondary schools was derived with the help of a sample survey of 574 schools under-

---

2. COLDATOS report.

3. DANE, "Investigación sobre Establecimientos Educativos," 1972 (processed).

4. Ministerio de Educación, "Estadísticas de la Educación Primaria Oficial" (processed).

5. This wage includes the Christmas bonus, which appears in the personal services item of the department budget.

6. The data referred to are given in the statistical appendix, Tables SA-18 and SA-19.

Table 3.8. *Public Contributions from All Sources to Public Primary Schools, 1973*

(thousands of pesos)

Department	Budgeted	Actual (estimated)
Antioquia	278,157	357,754
Atlántico	78,608	78,608
Bogotá, D. E.	300,108	349,838
Bolívar	65,537	68,707
Boyacá	107,873	111,109
Caldas	98,895	98,895
Cauca	56,978	66,095
Cesar	33,999	33,999
Choco	25,055	25,055
Córdoba	64,687	64,687
Cundinamarca	178,959	187,907
Huila	45,364	52,169
La Guajira	17,115	25,959
Magdalena	64,929	71,421
Meta	26,516	26,556
Nariño	65,656	65,656
N. Santander	77,577	77,577
Quindío	37,196	47,983
Risaralda	40,330	44,767
Santander	110,692	132,830
Sucre	33,841	43,656
Tolima	97,897	108,665
Valle del Cauca	160,851	165,651
Country total	2,066,824	2,304,544

Source: "Budgeted" data from COLDATOS report, p. 22.

taken by ICOLPE in 1972.[7] This survey provided data on the funding of each school as well as enrollment figures for 1972. In deriving the 1974 figure, the subsidy per student of 1972 was multiplied by 1.25 to allow for the 25 percent increase in teachers' salaries between both years.

Table 3.10 gives the estimates of the subsidy per student in secondary schools in urban areas, classified by city size and by

7. ICOLPE, "Costos de la Educación Media Oficial" 1972 (processed).

Table 3.9. *Public Primary Education: Estimated Enrollment, Total Subsidy, and Subsidy per Student, Classified by Stratum, 1973 and 1974*

Stratum	Enrollment	Total subsidy, 1973 (thousands of pesos)	Subsidy per student 1973 (pesos)	1974 (pesos)
Bogotá	288,245	348,125	1,207	1,449
Cali	102,826	56,711	551	662
Medellín	139,105	100,292	720	865
Barranquilla	62,335	48,240	773	928
5	47,741	33,027	691	830
6	45,227	37,249	823	988
7	59,922	52,691	879	1,055
8	42,090	27,540	654	785
9	75,193	49,903	663	796
10	34,022	24,231	712	855
11	123,830	98,824	767	920
12	47,521	24,581	517	620
13	33,976	26,047	548	658
14	18,626	9,107	488	586
15	28,731	21,780	758	909
16	25,217	21,597	856	1,028
17	48,918	31,549	644	774
18	41,241	31,249	757	909
19	65,832	61,291	931	1,117
20	41,034	34,487	840	1,009
21	28,877	27,398	948	1,038
22	87,878	70,522	802	963
23	52,620	42,011	798	958
24	48,489	35,128	724	869
25	49,371	36,861	746	895
26	39,352	35,086	891	1,070
27	53,789	40,937	761	913
28	65,592	40,038	610	732
29	82,638	46,268	559	671
30	65,190	48,614	745	895
31	76,311	56,179	736	883
32	87,266	69,313	794	953
33	61,898	63,619	1,027	1,233
34	79,238	62,952	794	953
35	57,097	42,820	749	900
36	—a	—a	—a	—a

Table 3.9. (*Continued*)

Stratum	Enrollment	Total subsidy, 1973 (*thousands of pesos*)	Subsidy per student	
			1973 (*pesos*)	1974 (*pesos*)
37	27,125	23,418	863	1,036
38	49,234	40,104	814	977
39	46,561	37,221	799	959
40	60,533	49,784	822	987
41	21,400	15,977	746	895
42	87,900	64,246	730	877
43	154,002	101,115	656	788
44	3,798	1,918	505	606
45	32,889	22,356	679	815
46	54,551	33,845	620	774
47	52,626	40,977	778	934
48	36,052	17,316	480	576
Country total	2,938,907	2,304,544	784	941

a. No schools outside the cabecera.
Source: COLDATOS report, p. 23–24.

Table 3.10. *Public Secondary Education:*
Estimated Subsidy per Student, Classified by Types of Schools, 1974

(pesos)

	Type of school				
	Bachillerato	Vocacional	Normalista	Comercial	Average
Large cities	3,725 (97.5)	5,031 (0.5)	6,369 (1.0)	3,451 (1.0)	3,773 (100.0)
Intermediate cities	3,744 (95.0)	5,067 (0.5)	5,020 (2.5)	2,631 (2.0)	3,760 (100.0)
Small towns	3,795 (83.8)	7,805 (0)	4,755 (13.8)	2,988 (2.4)	3,908 (100.0)

Note: Figures in parentheses are percentages of enrollment in each type of public secondary school.

Table 3.11. *Private Primary and Secondary Schools: Enrollment, Total Subsidy, and Subsidy per Student, 1974*

	Primary schools			Secondary schools		
	Enroll- ment[a] (thou- sands)	Total subsidy[b] (millions of pesos)	Subsidy per student (pesos)	Enroll- ment[a] (thou- sands)	Total subsidy[b] (millions of pesos)	Subsidy per student (pesos)
Large cities	73	4.3	58	90	56.5	628
Intermediate cities	41	4.8	117	51	35.6	698
Small towns	13	3.0	230	35	23.5	671
Rural areas	5	1.4	280	0	0	0
Country total	132	13.5	102	176	115.6	657

a. 1974 sample survey figures adjusted by the Ministry of Education totals. These figures refer only to enrollment in subsidized private schools.
b. National, departmental, and municipal budgets.

different types of schools. The average figure is the weighted average of the subsidy to different types of secondary schools.

Private primary and secondary schools

The item, "transfers," in the budget of the Ministry of Education presents data on individual transfers to private primary and secondary schools, as well as the location of each school. That item, together with the DANE directory of schools, provides the information necessary to classify private schools according to whether or not they receive subsidies. These figures from the Ministry of Education plus figures on transfers from departmental and municipal sources were used to derive the total subsidy figures in Table 3.11. The enrollment data, taken from the 1974 sample survey, refer only to enrollment in private schools that do receive subsidies.

Private and public universities

Subsidies to higher education were directly computed for 1974 in the COLDATOS report without a breakdown by regions. This breakdown becomes difficult when the location of the student's

Table 3.12. *Universities: Enrollment, Total Subsidy, and Subsidy per Student, 1974*

University	Enrollment (thousands)	Total subsidy (millions of pesos)	Subsidy per student (pesos)
Public	73	1,433.8	19,641
Private	76	58.9	775
Country total	149	1,492.7	10,018

Source: Data from COLDATOS report.

household differs from that of his school—a typical situation in higher education.

Table 3.12 presents figures for enrollment, total subsidy, and subsidy per student for public and private universities. Private universities include all nonpublic institutions, whether or not they receive subsidies.

Distribution of Subsidies across Income Groups

Table 3.13 summarizes the estimates of the subsidy per student derived earlier. The subsidy for each stratum for public primary schools was consolidated into broader categories since no logical intraregional breakdown fitted the variability of the subsidy figure.

Because of the method used, the estimated figures for primary and secondary public education shown in Table 3.13 do not necessarily correspond to the official totals. Fortunately, the difference is not significant.[8]

8. The differences between the estimated and official figures are shown below (in millions of pesos).

	Estimated	Official
Public primary	2,934.3	3,104.5
Public secondary	2,444.6	2,284.7

Official data are from the Ministerio de Educación, "Oficina Coordinadora de los FER y Oficina de Planeamiento de la Educación," (processed); Ministerio de Educación, "Ejecución Presupuestal" (processed).

Table 3.13. *Enrollment, Total Subsidy,*
and Estimated Subsidy per Student, 1974

Location	Educa-tional level	Enrollment (thousands) Public	Enrollment (thousands) Private[a]	Total subsidy (millions of pesos) Public	Total subsidy (millions of pesos) Private[a]	Subsidy per student (pesos) Public	Subsidy per student (pesos) Private[a]
Large cities	primary	746	73	819.8	4.3	1,099	58
	secondary	192	90	716.7	56.5	3,733	628
Inter-mediate cities	primary	556	41	480.9	4.8	865	117
	secondary	181	51	680.6	35.6	3,760	698
Small towns	primary	617	13	592.9	3.0	961	230
	secondary	150	35	586.2	23.5	3,908	671
Urban total	primary	1,919	127	1,893.6	12.1	987	94
	secondary	523	176	1,983.5	115.6	3,793	657
Rural total	primary	1,188	5	1,040.7	1.4	876	280
	secondary	118	0	461.1	0	3,908[b]	0
Country total	*primary*	*3,107*	*132*	*2,934.3*	*13.5*	*944[c]*	*102*
	secondary	*641*	*176*	*2,444.6*	*115.6*	*3,814*	*657*
	university	*73*	*76*	*1,433.8*	*58.9*	*19,641*	*775*
Subtotal		3,821	384	6,812.7	188.0		
Grand total		4,205		7,000.7			

a. Except in higher education, all private schools considered here are subsidized.
b. Same figure as for small towns.
c. This mean figure is different from the 941 figure arrived at in Table 3.9, given that the 1974 urban-rural weight is being used.

In public education, which accounts for 97 percent of the total subsidy to education, differences in the subsidy per student are not significant across regions—at least not at the level of approximation at which these figures must be interpreted. In the case of public primary education, large cities have the highest subsidy, 1,099 pesos; for urban areas the figure is 987 pesos; and for rural areas 876—a 13 percent difference.

In public education, the largest variation in the subsidy is across educational levels. The subsidy per student in secondary education is approximately four times that in primary education; the subsidy in higher education is twenty times that in primary and five times that in secondary.

In private primary schools the subsidy varies according to the location of the school, becoming larger the smaller the size of the city. Since enrollment in these schools is low (approximately 4 percent of the total enrollment in primary schools), however, this variation is not significant in determining the total distributive effect of the subsidy.

Subsidies per household

Table 3.14 presents figures on the subsidy per household, according to location and income quintile. The mean annual subsidy per household in the country is 1,947 pesos or $70.50. The subsidy for primary education becomes substantially larger for the lower-income groups. For higher education the subsidy is much greater for the higher-income groups. The net result is a more or less constant subsidy per household across quintiles. In other words, the highly distributive subsidy to primary education is almost exactly compensated for by the regressive subsidy to higher education. The subsidy to secondary education is slightly higher for the middle-income quintiles.

Rural households receive a substantially smaller subsidy from primary and secondary education. The difference becomes more marked in the lower quintiles; rural households in the poorest 40 percent of households receive half the subsidy of urban households in the same group because of the low enrollment rate in low-income families in rural areas. Within urban areas, the mean subsidy per household is lower for large cities than for small ones because of the relatively greater enrollment in unsubsidized private schools in the larger cities.

Subsidy per capita

The constancy of the subsidy across quintiles, when defined per household, disappears when expressed in per capita terms: that is, the subsidy per household divided by the number of individuals in the family. This comparison is shown in Table 3.15. Since the subsidy per household is more or less constant, the variation in the subsidy per capita follows the variation in family size across income quintiles. The subsidy per capita is almost 75 percent larger for households in the richest quintile than for those in the poorest.

Table 3.14. *Education Subsidy per Household, 1974*
(pesos)

Income quintile (poorest to richest)	Large cities			Intermediate cities			Small towns		
	Pri-mary	Sec-ondary	Total	Pri-mary	Sec-ondary	Total	Pri-mary	Sec-ondary	Total
1	1,642	772	2,414	1,459	1,163	2,622	1,317	998	2,315
2	1,435	1,182	2,617	1,166	1,590	2,756	1,288	1,154	2,442
3	873	1,089	1,962	992	1,109	2,101	1,205	842	2,047
4	861	797	1,658	613	1,252	1,865	593	1,323	1,916
5	278	368	646	235	760	995	338	1,440	1,778
Country average	784	729	1,513	769	1,146	1,915	1,062	1,095	2,157

Note: To obtain dollar figures, divide by 27.6.

Subsidy as a percentage of income

Tables 3.16 and 3.17 show the subsidy per household expressed as a percentage of the annual household income reported in the 1974 sample survey. Table 3.16 shows that the typical Colombian household receives a subsidy from the educational sector equal to 5 percent of its annual income. For the poorest quintile, the subsidy is equivalent to 18.4 percent, whereas for the highest it is only 1.9 percent. Table 3.17 shows that even if primary and secondary education only are included, urban households receive almost twice the percentage subsidy received by rural households

Table 3.15. *Education Subsidy Figures per Household and per Capita*

Income quintile (poorest to richest)	Subsidy per household (pesos)	Family size	Subsidy per capita (pesos)
1	1,921	6.87	280
2	1,961	5.99	327
3	1,810	5.38	336
4	1,950	4.80	406
5	2,064	4.25	486
Country average	1,947	5.50	354

Urban areas			Rural areas			Country average			
Pri-mary	Sec-ondary	Total	Pri-mary	Sec-ondary	Total	Pri-mary	Sec-ondary	Uni-versity	Total
1,464	969	2,433	1,103	273	1,376	1,305	598	18	1,921
1,317	1,284	2,601	858	273	1,131	1,089	776	96	1,961
993	1,039	2,032	633	391	1,024	835	751	224	1,810
715	1,070	1,785	359	469	828	589	872	489	1,950
263	565	828	237	352	589	252	555	1,257	2,064
854	925	1,779	754	352	1,106	816	718	413	1,947

in the same quintile. Although the subsidy is larger for urban households in the same quintile, the mean is larger for the rural area (4.8 percent) than for the urban area (3.7 percent). This is because more rural households are in the lower-income quintiles, where percentage subsidies are largest.

The reliability of these percentage figures is proportional to the reliability of the income figures reported by households in the sample survey: that is, less reliable for rural areas and for higher-income groups. The sample survey yielded an annual household income of 38,904 pesos, equal to a dollar per capita income of

Table 3.16. *Total Education Subsidy per Household as a Percentage of Reported Household Annual Income*

Income quintile (poorest to richest)	Reported mean annual income (pesos)	Subsidies (percentage)			
		Primary	Secondary	University	Total
1	10,368	12.6	5.8	—	18.4
2	17,820	6.1	4.4	0.5	11.0
3	25,032	3.3	3.0	0.9	7.2
4	36,912	1.6	2.4	1.3	5.3
5	104,388	0.2	0.5	1.2	1.9
Country average	38,904	2.1	1.8	1.1	5.0

Table 3.17. *Primary and Secondary Education Subsidy per Household as a Percentage of Household Annual Income, by Urban and Rural Regions, 1974*

	Urban			Rural		
Income quintile (poorest to richest)	Reported mean annual income (pesos)	Number of families (percentage)	Subsidy (percentage)	Reported mean annual income (pesos)	Number of families (percentage)	Subsidy (percentage)
1	10,272	15.0	23.7	10,452	27.9	13.2
2	18,024	16.8	14.4	17,604	26.9	6.4
3	26,052	17.8	7.8	23,736	22.7	4.3
4	38,712	22.5	4.6	32,808	15.8	2.5
5	108,768	27.9	0.8	74,484	6.7	0.8
Country average	48,262	100.0	3.7	23,214	100.0	4.8

$256;[9] the national accounts figures show a GNP per capita for 1974 twice as large. Although there are conceptual reasons why the household survey would yield lower-income figures, the size of the difference suggests that the reported income figures represent an underestimate. This qualification must be considered in interpreting the subsidy expressed as a percentage of household income.

Distribution of subsidies and distribution of income

Table 3.18 compares the distribution of the subsidy with the distribution of income. The total subsidy to education represents 11.2 percent of total government expenditure and 2.2 percent of the GNP. Primary education accounts for 42.1 percent of the total subsidy—almost twice the subsidy to higher education.

Figure 3.1 presents Lorenz curves for the distribution of the subsidy compared with the distribution of income. The horizontal axis shows the accumulated percentage of households, ordered according to household per capita income; the vertical axis, the accumulated percentages of subsidy and total income. The Lorenz curve for the total subsidy almost coincides with the 45 degree

9. With a mean family size of 5.5 and an exchange rate of 27.6 pesos to the dollar (1974).

Figure 3.1. *Distribution of Income and of Subsidies for Education*

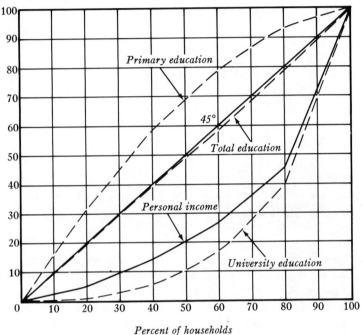

Percent of income/
Percent of subsidy

Percent of households

diagonal; it is clearly more evenly distributed than personal income. The line above the diagonal, representing the distribution of the subsidy to primary education, shows a distribution in favor of lower-income households: lower-income families receive a higher share of the subsidy than the percentage they represent in the total number of families. The subsidy to higher education, however, not only favors higher-income households (the line is below the diagonal), but it also shows a stronger inequality than the distribution of personal income: lower-income households receive a smaller share of that subsidy than of the total income.

When the Lorenz lines are plotted for the percentage of individuals (instead of for the percentage of households), all distribu-

Table 3.18. *Distribution of the Subsidy to Education
and Distribution of Personal Income, 1974*
(percentage)

Income quintile (*poorest to richest*)	House-holds	Indi-viduals	Subsidy for education				
			Primary	Sec-ondary	Univer-sity	Average	Income[a]
1	20	25.1	32.1	16.8	0.8	19.8	5.2
2	20	22.7	26.7	21.8	4.6	20.2	9.1
3	20	19.4	20.5	21.2	10.7	18.6	12.6
4	20	17.4	14.5	24.6	23.5	20.1	18.7
5	20	15.4	6.2	15.6	60.4	21.3	54.4
As a percentage of:							
Total education subsidy			42.1	36.6	21.3	100.0	
Total government expenditure[b]			4.7	4.1	2.4	11.2	
GNP[c]			0.9	0.8	0.5	2.2	

a. Income distribution from the 1974 sample survey.
b. Corresponds to direct expenditures by the central government plus contributions to decentralized agencies. The total is 62.7 billion pesos. Contraloría General de la República de Colombia. "Informe Financiero de 1974," p. 818.
c. The GNP equals 322.6 billion pesos (International Financial Statistics).

tion lines show a stronger inequality. In this particular case, the relation of the lines to each other remains the same. Plotted for the population, the total subsidy line lies below the 45 degree diagonal; 25.1 percent of the poorest population receives 19.8 percent of the subsidy, whereas the richest 15.4 percent of the population receives 21.3 percent. These findings are compared with results from earlier studies in the following appendix.

Appendix. Comparisons with Other Studies

Several studies on the distributive effect of government expenditure, particularly in education, have been made in Colombia. It is interesting to compare the earlier findings with those presented in this chapter.

Urrutia and Sandoval

In their pioneer work on this subject, Miguel Urrutia and Clara Elsa de Sandoval attempted to derive income distribution data corrected by taxation and by the effect of government expenditure.[10] The study was undertaken for 1966, using 1964 income distribution data. The authors tried to allocate the public subsidy to education among income groups.

In the absence of direct survey data on school enrollment, Urrutia and Sandoval had to decide on a method of allocating enrollment according to income group. For this purpose, all children of primary school age (7 to 11) and secondary school age (12 to 17) were classified into three groups: those not enrolled; those enrolled in private schools; and those enrolled in public schools. The children not enrolled were allocated to the poorest-income deciles (tenths); those in private schools to the richest deciles; and those in public schools to the remaining deciles.

The expenditure in higher education was distributed by classifying students at the National University according to their parents' level of schooling[11] and by using the 1964 census to classify the male population 40 to 59 years old by level of schooling. Assuming a correspondence between the distribution of individuals in that age bracket classified by schooling and the population classified by per capita income (that is, if x percent of the individuals in that age bracket have 0 to 2 years of schooling, it means that they belong to households representing the bottom x percent of individuals classified according to per capita income), it was possible to classify the enrollment in universities according to income groups.

Table 3.19 shows the resulting distribution of subsidies according to quintiles defined by the distribution of the population by per capita income. The figures in parentheses are figures from the present study expressed for quintiles of households, not population, in the distribution of personal income. Because the poorest and richest quintiles of households account for 25.1 and 15.4 percent of the population, respectively, the figures in parentheses for these quintiles must be multiplied by 0.8 and 1.3, respectively, for comparison with those in the Urrutia-Sandoval study.[12]

The 1974 survey shows a substantially more progressive sub-

---

10. Miguel Urrutia and Clara E. de Sandoval, "Política Fiscal y Distribución del Ingreso en Colombia," Revista Banco de la República, July 1974.

11. German Rama, "Origen Social de la Población Universitaria," Universidad Nacional, August 1969.

12. The correction factor for the middle-income quintiles approaches 1.

Table 3.19. *Distribution of Education Subsidies,*
1966, Urrutia-Sandoval

Income quintiles (poorest to richest)	Subsidies for education							
	Pri- mary	Sec- ondary	Uni- versity	Total	Primary	Sec- ondary	Univer- sity	Average
	(millions of pesos, 1966)					*(percentage)*		
1	145	0	3	148	15.7	0	1.1	9.9
					(32.1)	(16.8)	(0.8)	(19.8)
2	170	0	10	180	18.5	0	3.8	12.1
					(26.7)	(21.8)	(4.6)	(20.2)
3	194	0	16	210	21.1	0	6.0	14.1
					(20.5)	(21.2)	(10.7)	(18.6)
4	267	144	16	427	29.0	47.5	6.0	28.7
					(14.5)	(24.6)	(23.5)	(20.1)
5	145	159	221	525	15.7	52.5	83.1	35.2
					(6.2)	(15.6)	(60.4)	(21.3)
Country total	921	303	266	1,490	100.0	100.0	100.0	100.0

Note: Values in parentheses refer to relative comparable figures from the 1974 survey.
Source: Miguel Urrutia and Clara E. de Sandoval, "Política Fiscal y Distribución del Ingreso en Colombia."

sidy than the 1966 results. Two factors are behind this difference: a much higher enrollment rate in primary education for the poorest quintiles and a much larger enrollment rate in secondary education, which the 1966 study assumed to be nil for the poorest 60 percent. Part of the difference arises from the assumptions used in the 1966 study, where all nonenrolled children were allocated to the poorest-income groups; the implicit relation between the enrollment rate and the income level resulting from this assumption has an exaggerated slope and, for primary education, a discontinuity. The second source of difference is that the enrollment rate in the poorest-income groups may have sharply increased between 1966 and 1974.

Jallade

The distribution of public expenditures in education, including investment, was also estimated for 1970 by Jallade as part of a comprehensive study comparing the distribution of educational

Table 3.20. *Distribution of Education Subsidies,
1970, Jallade*

Household income (thousands of pesos)	Households[a] (percentage)	Percentage of subsidy			Average (percentage)
		Primary	Secondary	University	
0–6	19.0	11.0	1.7	—	5.9
	(20.0)	(32.1)	(16.8)	(0.8)	(19.8)
6–12	20.2	17.9	1.7	0.9	9.5
	(20.0)	(26.7)	(21.8)	(4.6)	(20.2)
12–24	24.9	32.5	21.8	7.6	23.7
	(20.0)	(20.5)	(21.2)	(10.7)	(18.6)
24–60	22.9	31.0	50.9	40.7	38.7
	(20.0)	(14.5)	(24.6)	(23.5)	(20.1)
Over 60	13.0	7.6	23.9	50.8	22.2
	(20.0)	(6.2)	(15.6)	(60.4)	(21.3)

Note: Values in parentheses refer to quintiles of households as ordered by household per capita income from the 1974 survey.

benefits with the distribution of taxation. Comparisons were made across income groups as well as regions.[13]

Enrollment data for urban areas were obtained by using the 1970 DANE household survey.[14] Direct data on enrollment were available for children age 12 or older. For children under 12, enrollment by income group was derived by comparing the number of grades passed (as reported in the survey) with the age of the child; this comparison was then used to classify children as still enrolled or as dropouts. For the rural areas, the known total of enrolled students in primary education was allocated across income groups by assuming that all households have the same number of children in the 5 to 25 year age bracket and that enrollment ratio is a function of income.

Table 3.20 presents the distribution of subsidies obtained in Jallade's study, allocated across families according to household income. The values in parentheses are from the present study,

13. Jean-Pierre Jallade, *Public Expenditures on Education and Income Distribution in Colombia*, World Bank Staff Occasional Papers, no. 18 (Baltimore: Johns Hopkins University Press, 1974).

14. DANE, "Household survey," 1970.

Table 3.21. *Comparison of Enrollment per Household in Primary Education, Jallade and Sample Survey*

Yearly household income (thousands of pesos)	Urban areas		Rural areas	
	Percentage of households	Enrollment per household	Percentage of households	Enrollment per household
Jallade, 1970				
0–6			45.1	0.58
	14.7	0.76		(0.58)
		(0.69)		
6–12			31.9	0.89
				(0.89)
12–24	30.3	0.91	16.5	1.27
		(0.79)		(1.27)
24–60	34.3	0.96	6.5	1.93
		(0.74)		(1.93)
Over 60	20.7	0.82	0	0
		(0.22)		
Country total	100.0	0.90	100.0	0.91
		(0.64)		(0.91)

Quintile in country income distribution	Urban areas		Rural areas	
	Percentage of households	Enrollment per household	Percentage of households	Enrollment per household
1974 sample survey				
1	15.0	1.68	27.9	1.28
		(1.48)		(1.26)
2	16.8	1.51	26.9	0.97
		(1.33)		(0.98)
3	17.8	1.25	22.7	0.75
		(1.00)		(0.72)
4	22.5	0.92	15.8	0.44
		(0.72)		(0.41)
5	27.9	0.57	6.7	0.30
		(0.26)		(0.27)
Country total	100.0	1.10	100.0	0.88
		(0.86)		(0.86)

Note: Figures in parentheses show enrollment in public school.

Table 3.22. *Comparison of Enrollment per Household in Secondary Education, Jallade and Sample Survey*

Yearly household income (thousands of pesos)	Urban areas		Country average	
	Percentage of households	Enrollment per household	Percentage of households	Enrollment per household
	Jallade, 1970			
0–12	14.7	0.04 (0.04)	39.2	0.01 (0.01)
12–24	30.3	0.15 (0.13)	24.9	0.11 (0.09)
24–60	34.3	0.40 (0.26)	22.9	0.36 (0.23)
Over 60	20.7	0.73 (0.17)	13.0	0.71 (0.16)
Country total	100.0	0.34 (0.17)	100.0	0.21 (0.10)

Quintile in country income distribution	Urban areas		Rural areas		Country average	
	Percentage of households	Enrollment per household	Percentage of households	Enrollment per household	Percentage of households	Enrollment per household
	1974 sample survey					
1	15.0	0.43 (0.24)	27.9	0.09 (0.07)	20	0.24 (0.15)
2	16.8	0.47 (0.33)	26.9	0.10 (0.07)	20	0.28 (0.20)
3	17.8	0.48 (0.26)	32.7	0.11 (0.10)	20	0.31 (0.19)
4	22.5	0.53 (0.27)	15.8	0.14 (0.12)	20	0.42 (0.22)
5	27.9	0.57 (0.13)	6.7	0.11 (0.09)	20	0.50 (0.13)
Country total	100.0	0.50 (0.23)	100.0	0.12 (0.09)	100	0.35 (0.18)

Note: Figures in parentheses show the enrollment in public schools.

where quintiles of households are ordered by household per capita income.

If, as appears from the 1974 study, family size is a negative function of household per capita income, then families in low-income quintiles will have more children than higher-income quintiles when quintiles of households are ordered by per capita income instead of household income. If this negative function is strong enough, sharp differences in the distribution of educational subsidies can be expected when families are ordered and quintiles are defined by per capita income instead of by household income. This helps to explain the differences in Table 3.20, where poorer families receive a much smaller share of subsidies when they are ordered by household income instead of by household per capita income.

The source of those differences can be seen more clearly in Tables 3.21 and 3.22, which show the enrollment per household in primary and secondary education. Because most of the subsidy goes to public education, the difference in the values in parentheses across income groups is the major determinant of the distribution of that subsidy. According to the 1974 sample survey, the enrollment per household in primary education, particularly in public schools, increases sharply for lower-income groups when they are ordered by household per capita income. The reverse is found in Jallade's study when families are ordered by household income, particularly in rural areas. Part of this difference could result from the effect of family size on the ordering; it could also reflect genuine differences in enrollment rates for low-income families of comparable per capita income.

Chapter 4

The Distribution
of Public Subsidies for Health

THE COLOMBIAN HEALTH SYSTEM has three components: the National Health System (NHS), the Colombian Institute of Social Security (ICSS), and the Social Security of the Public Sector (Cajas Publicas).

The National Health System is the central public health system of the country. In theory, every individual is entitled to use its services. It is run by the Ministry of Health and is financed by funds from the central government, national lotteries, and the contributions of departments and municipalities. Three types of institutions provide services: public hospitals; health centers with at least one full-time doctor; and puestos de salud (smaller health centers), which usually have only a part-time doctor.[1]

The Colombian Institute of Social Security (ICSS) not only administers retirement and pension funds, but also provides health services to member employees in the private sector through hospitals and health centers. Funding for the ICSS comes from three sources: contributions from the Ministry of Health and compulsory payments made by both employers and employees.

The third health system is made up of the various Social Security branches that serve employees in the public sector. The most important of these are the Caja Nacional de Previsión

1. On the average, there are 1.88 doctors, 0.81 dentists, and 3.7 auxiliares (a type of nurse) to a health center. An average puesto de salud has 0.53 doctors and 1.06 auxiliaries.

(CAJANAL) and the Caja de Previsión de Comunicaciones (CAPRECOM). This system is financed by contributions from the central government, public agencies employing workers belonging to the system, and the employees themselves. It also maintains hospitals and health centers.

Total Subsidy Received by Households

The method used to derive subsidies for health was largely determined by the type of data obtained in the 1974 sample survey on household consumption of health services according to location and income groups. The relation between the survey data and the structure of the health system is illustrated in Figure 4.1.

Sources of the subsidies

Table 4.1 gives figures for the flow of funds shown in Figure 4.1, where A, B, and C are contributions to different institutions of the National Health System, and D and E are contributions from the Social Security System to the hospitals belonging to ICSS and Cajas Publicas.[2] For the Social Security System these figures do not represent the subsidy received by the beneficiaries

---

2. Flow A was derived from the COLDATOS report, based on data from the Ministry of Health. (Cardex Ministerio de Salud: Presupuesto de Hospitales Oficiales y Mixtos. See COLDATOS report.) Flows B and C were estimated by using 1969 data on the running cost of health centers and an estimate of costs for puestos de salud, based on size of staff. Table SA-20 in the statistical appendix, shows the cost of each health center (with and without beds) for 1969, adjusted for the increase in the price level between 1969 and 1974.

The cost of maintaining each puesto de salud (Table SA-21) was derived by comparing the wage bill for the average puesto staff in 1969 (0.53 doctors, 1.06 auxiliaries) with the average wage bill for a health center. The 1969 figure was again adjusted by the change in the price level between 1969 and 1974 (103 percent). Table SA-22 shows the total cost of operating the puestos, by location. The cost of each puesto is assumed to be the same in all locations; thus the total subsidy becomes proportional to the number of puestos in each location.

Flow D is derived from ICSS figures in the COLDATOS report (*Informe Estadistico ICSS*). Flow E includes 259.8 million pesos from CAJANAL (Item, "Prestaciones Médicas," of *Presupuesto de Ingreso y Rentas*) and 39 million from CAPRECOM (Item, "Servicios Médicos," *Presupuesto de Entidades Descentralizadas, Informe Financiero de 1973, República de Colombia*). The breakdown of Flow E by location was based on the percent distribution shown in the COLDATOS report and on the 1969 INPES study on health institutions (INPES: *Censo de Instituciones Hospitalarias*, 1970).

Figure 4.1. *Colombian Health System*

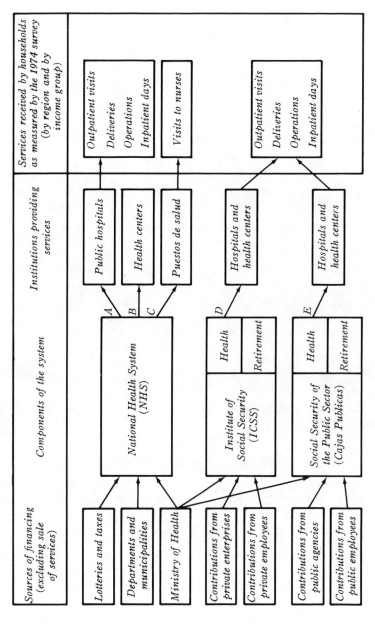

Table 4.1. *Funding Received by Health Institutions, 1974*
(millions of pesos)

Health system and institution	Large cities	Inter- mediate cities	Small towns	Urban total	Rural areas	Country total
National Health System						
Hospitals (A)	283.5	339.4	381.7	1,004.6	13.8	1,018.4
Health centers (B)	106.4	54.5	54.8	215.7	22.3	238.0
Puestos (C)	1.2	7.3	34.5	43.0	57.5	100.5
Social Security System						
ICSS (D)	954.2	367.3	142.1	1,436.6	5.1	1,468.7
Cajas (E)	225.1	22.9	12.8	260.8	38.0	298.8
Total funding	*1,570.4*	*791.4*	*625.9*	*2,987.7*	*136.7*	*3,124.4*

Sources: See text (note 2) and Figure 4.1.

of the system. The subsidy is smaller, since it must exclude the fraction of that funding financed by the laborers themselves.

Excluding indebtedness, the sources of financing of the Social Security System are:

Contributions	ICSS (percentage)	Cajas (percentage)
Ministry of Health	4.8 ⎫	61.9 ⎫
Private enterprises (ICSS)	⎬ 72.0	⎬ 70.8
or public agencies (Cajas)	67.2 ⎭	8.9 ⎭
Employees	28.0	29.2

According to these figures, the contribution of workers to the ICSS is 29 percent of the total contribution of workers and employees (0.280/0.952). It also coincides approximately with the percentage contribution fixed by law, namely, 3.5 and 7.0 percent of the wage for workers and employers, respectively. Thus, the contribution from labor is 33 percent of the total contribution. The contribution of labor to the Cajas Publicas is 29 percent, if 70.8 percent is defined as the contribution of the (public) employer.

A rigorous definition of the subsidy should exclude the real (not legal) contribution of workers: that is, the difference between the wage that would have prevailed without the system and the new net wage received by labor. This incidence depends not only on labor supply and demand, but also on the value placed by workers on the services provided by the system. This valuation will in turn affect the new (post-system) supply price of labor and thus the new equilibrium wage.

In the appendix to this chapter, a simple framework for evaluating the real incidence borne by labor is presented. It is shown that the larger the ratio of the elasticity of labor supply relative to labor demand, the smaller the incidence borne by labor. If that ratio is 2, and workers place zero value on the services they receive, the real incidence becomes equal to the legal incidence; if workers value the services in an amount equal to one quarter of the contribution of both labor and employers, the real incidence borne by labor is 0.5. If a reasonable range of values is used—a ratio of elasticities between 2 and 5 and a valuation of services ranging from 0.10 to 0.5 times the total contribution—the real incidence fluctuates between 0.4 and 0.6. A value of 0.5 will be used for the calculation: namely, an economic incidence larger than the legal figure of 0.29 discussed earlier. Thus the subsidy in the ICSS system becomes equal to 0.524 [0.048 + (0.5)(0.952)] times the contributions shown in Table 4.1. In the case of the Cajas Publicas, if the nonlabor contribution is defined as the contribution of the (public) employer, the subsidy becomes 0.5 times the contribution shown in Table 4.1.

The estimated subsidies are summarized in Table 4.2. The total health subsidy for 1974 becomes 2,276.1 million pesos, one-third of the subsidy for education, (7,000.6 million pesos). It represents 3.6 percent of total government expenditure and 0.7 percent of the Colombian GNP.

Subsidy classified by type of health service

The next step is to classify the subsidy figures by type of service, using the same classification as the 1974 sample survey. For this an independent estimate of the relative cost of providing these services is required.

The only data source for the relative unit cost of health services is a 1974 study of the ICSS hospitals.[3] The estimated costs, in terms

3. *Estudio de Costos de Servicios Médicos.* ICSS, 1974.

Table 4.2. *Estimated Total Subsidy Received by Households, 1974*
(millions of pesos)

Health system and institution	Large cities	Intermediate cities	Small towns	Urban total	Rural areas	Country total
National Health Service						
Hospitals (A)	283.5	339.4	381.7	1,004.6	13.8	1,018.4
Health centers (B)	106.4	54.5	54.8	215.7	22.3	238.0
Puestos (C)	1.2	7.3	34.5	43.0	57.5	100.5
Social Security System						
ICSS[a]	500.0	192.5	74.5	767.0	2.7	769.7
Cajas [b]	112.6	11.5	6.4	130.5	19.0	149.5
Total subsidy	*1,003.7*	*605.2*	*551.9*	*2,160.8*	*115.3*	*2,276.1*

Column header spanning: *Location of institution* covers Large cities, Intermediate cities, Small towns.

a. Figures are 52.4 percent of those in Table 4.1.
b. Figures are 50 percent of those in Table 4.1.

of the cost of one outpatient visit, are as follows: 1 delivery equals 1.17 outpatient visits; 1 operation equals 29.5; and 1 inpatient day equals 4. If these figures are representative for all hospitals, the number of services provided by all types of hospitals can be expressed in terms of equivalent outpatient visits. The percentage distribution of each service, in equivalent outpatient visits, can thereafter be used to distribute the total subsidy. Tables 4.3, 4.4, and 4.5 show the number of services provided by the three classes of hospitals in 1974 in terms of equivalent outpatient visits and the distribution of the subsidy according to the percentage distribution of the visits.[4]

4. Data on the number of services provided by ICSS in 1974 were available from official statistical reports (*Informe Estadistico*, ICSS). For the hospitals belonging to the National Health System and Cajas Publicas, 1969 data from the INPES study were used. The number of services provided in 1969 was expanded by the increase in the total number of outpatient visits, for which 1974 data were available. In other words, it was assumed that all services grew at the same rate as outpatient visits. Although this expansion is not necessary to derive the percentage distribution of the subsidy, it allows for some comparison with the absolute number of services reported by households in the sample survey.

Table 4.3. *National Health System Hospitals:*
Number of Services Provided and the Distribution of the Subsidy, 1974

	Location of institution					
Services	*Large cities*	*Inter- mediate cities*	*Small towns*	*Urban total*	*Rural areas*	*Country total*
Services provided in 1974 (thousands) Number of services provided						
Outpatient visits	1,193	906	1,942	4,041	98	4,139
Deliveries	78	55	60	193	2	195
Operations	125	63	31	219	1	220
Inpatient days	1,657	2,189	2,075	5,921	110	6,031
Number of services in equivalent outpatient visits[a]						
Outpatient visits	1,193	906	1,942	4,041	98	4,139
Deliveries	91.3	64.4	70.2	225.9	2.3	228.2
Operations	3,687.5	1,858.5	914.5	6,460.5	29.5	6,490
Inpatient days	6,628	8,756	8,300	23,684	440	24,124
Total	11,599.8	11,584.9	11,226.7	34,411.4	569.8	34,981.2
Distribution of the 1974 subsidy (millions of pesos)						
Outpatient days	29.2	26.5	66.0	121.7	2.4	124.1
Deliveries	2.2	1.9	2.4	6.5	0.1	6.6
Operations	90.1	54.4	31.1	175.6	0.7	176.3
Inpatient days	162.0	256.6	282.2	700.8	10.6	711.4
Total	283.5	339.4	381.7	1,004.6	13.8	1,018.4

a. The cost of 1 delivery equals the cost of 1.17 outpatient visits; of 1 operation equals 29.5; and of 1 in-patient day equals 4.
Source: Data from INPES study, 1969.

Table 4.6 summarizes data on the subsidy by type of service and type of health system. The values for the ICSS and Cajas Publicas have been combined as a total figure for the Social Security System. The figures for health centers were not broken down by type of service.

In the case of National Health System hospitals, almost 75 percent of the subsidy goes to finance inpatient care. In the Social Security System, the subsidy is more or less evenly spread over outpatient visits and inpatient care, with approximately 40 percent of the subsidy going to each type of service.

Table 4.4. ICSS *Hospitals: Number of Services Provided and the Distribution of the Subsidy, 1974*

	Location of institution					
Services	*Large cities*	*Inter-mediate cities*	*Small towns*	*Urban total*	*Rural areas*	*Country total*
Services provided in 1974 (thousands)						
Number of services provided						
Outpatient visits	4,696	2,507	884	8,087	37	8,121
Deliveries	47	20	7	74	—	74
Operations	70	22	10	102	—	102
Inpatient days	954	467	156	1,577	5	1,582
Number of services in equivalent outpatient days[a]						
Outpatient days	4,696	2,507	884	8,087	34	8,121
Deliveries	55	23.4	8.2	86.6	—	86.6
Operations	2,065	649	295	3,009	—	3,009
Inpatient days	3,816	1,868	624	6,308	20	6,328
Total	10,632	5,047.4	11,811.2	17,490.6	54	17,544.6
Distribution of the 1974 subsidy (millions of pesos)						
Outpatient days	220.8	95.6	36.4	352.8	1.7	354.5
Deliveries	2.6	0.9	0.3	3.8	—	3.8
Operations	97.1	24.8	12.1	134	—	134
Inpatient days	179.5	71.2	25.7	276.4	1.0	277.4
Total	500.0	192.5	74.5	767.0	2.7	769.7

a. The cost of 1 delivery equals the cost of 1.17 outpatient visits; of 1 operation equals 29.5; and of 1 inpatient day equals 4.
Source: Data from *Informe Estadistico*, ICSS, 1974.

Consumption of Services and Distribution of Subsidies across Income Groups

The 1974 sample survey provides data on the consumption of different services as reported by households. These figures can

Table 4.5. *Cajas Publicas Hospitals: Number of Services Provided for 1969 and Distribution of the Subsidy in 1974*

	Location of institution					
Services	*Large cities*	*Inter-mediate cities*	*Small towns*	*Urban total*	*Rural areas*	*Country total*
Services provided in 1974 (thousands)						
Number of services provided						
Outpatient visits	348.9	68.2	25.7	442.8	86.6	529.4
Deliveries	5.7	0.3	0.1	6.1	1.5	7.6
Operations	13.6	0.7	0.2	14.5	0.5	15.0
Inpatient days	291.5	12.6	16.2	320.3	41.0	361.3
Number of services in equivalent outpatient days[a]						
Outpatient days	348.9	68.2	25.7	442.8	86.6	529.4
Deliveries	6.7	0.4	0.1	7.2	1.8	9.0
Operations	401.2	20.6	5.9	427.7	14.8	442.5
Inpatient days	1,165.6	50.4	64.8	1,280.8	163.9	1,444.7
Total	1,922.4	139.6	96.5	2,158.5	267.1	2,425.6
Distribution of the 1974 subsidy (millions of pesos)						
Outpatient days	20.5	5.6	1.7	27.8	6.2	34.0
Deliveries	0.3	0.1	0.1	0.5	0.1	0.6
Operations	23.5	1.7	0.4	25.6	1.0	26.6
Inpatient days	68.3	4.1	4.2	76.6	11.7	88.3
Total	112.6	11.5	6.4	130.5	19.0	149.5

a. The cost of 1 delivery equals the cost of 1.17 outpatient visits; of 1 operation equals 29.5; and of 1 in-patient day equals 4.

Source: Data from INPES study, 1969.

now be compared with those reported by the health institutions themselves.

Allocation of subsidies to urban and rural households

This comparison is necessary to allocate the subsidy between urban and rural households since an important fraction of rural

Table 4.6. *Public Subsidies to Health Institutions,*
Classified by Location of the Institution, 1974
(millions of pesos)

Health system and service	Large cities	Inter-mediate cities	Small towns	Urban total	Rural areas	Country total
			Location of institution			
National Health System						
Hospitals						
Outpatient visits	29.2	26.5	66.0	121.7	2.4	124.1
Deliveries	2.2	1.9	2.4	6.5	0.1	6.6
Operations	90.1	54.4	31.1	175.6	0.7	176.3
Inpatient days	162.0	256.6	282.2	700.8	10.6	711.4
Health centers	107.6	61.8	89.3	258.7	79.8	338.5
Social Security System						
Hospitals						
Outpatient visits	241.3	101.2	38.1	380.6	7.9	388.5
Deliveries	2.9	1.0	0.4	4.3	0.1	4.4
Operations	120.6	26.5	12.5	159.6	1.0	160.6
Inpatient days	247.8	75.3	29.9	353.0	12.7	365.7

households' consumption takes place in urban institutions. The comparison of the two sets of data is shown in Table 4.7.

If an important part of the services provided in urban areas is consumed by rural households, an excess supply of services in urban areas (defined as an excess of services provided over services consumed by households located in that area) and an excess demand of services in rural areas (defined as an excess of services consumed by households located in the area over the ones provided by the institutions in the area) would be expected. Although the data in Table 4.7 seem to demonstrate this, the size of the excess supply in urban areas (particularly for the Social Security System) is substantially larger than the excess demand in rural areas. In other words, the country total figures reported by the health institutions are larger than the country total figures reported by households. The largest difference—in outpatient visits to institutions of the Social Security System—may occur because the number of visits reported by households refers only to visits to

Table 4.7. *Number of Services Provided in Hospitals*
(*Reported by Health Institutions*) *and Consumed by Households*
(*Reported in the 1974 Sample Survey*)
(thousands)

Health system and service	Large cities	Inter- mediate cities	Small towns	Urban total	Rural areas	Country total
National Health System						
Outpatient days	1,193	906	1,942	4,041	98	4,139
	(891)	(1,040)	(939)	(2,870)	(1,204)	(4,074)
Deliveries	78	55	60	193	2	195
	(34)	(36)	(30)	(100)	(76)	(176)
Operations	125	63	31	219	1	220
	(49)	(24)	(11)	(84)	(25)	(109)
Inpatient days	1,657	2,189	2,075	5,921	110	6,031
	(1,611)	(1,080)	(660)	(3,351)	(2,679)	(6,030)
Social Security System[a]						
Outpatient visits	4,696	2,507	884	8,087	34	8,121
	(1,510)	(1,129)	(411)	(3,050)	(258)	(3,288)
Deliveries	47	20	7	74	—	74
	(22)	(16)	(8)	(46)	(9)	(55)
Operations	70	22	10	101	—	101
	(16)	(5)	(1)	(22)	—	(22)
Inpatient days	954	467	156	1,577	5	1,582
	(778)	(230)	(100)	(1,158)	—	(1,158)

Note: Figures are reported according to the locations of the institution and of the household. Figures reported by households are in parentheses.
a. Figures reported by institutions include only hospitals belonging to the ICSS system.

physicians, whereas the figures reported by the institutions refer to visits to paramedical personnel as well.

For the purposes of the study, the number of services received by rural households in urban areas will be assumed to be equal to the excess demand figures for the rural areas in Table 4.7. These figures appear in the first column of Table 4.8, where they are allocated to institutions classified by city size. The rural excess demand was allocated according to the excess supply figures in each urban stratum, from small towns up to large cities. Obviously, the last number allocated need not coincide with the excess

Table 4.8. *Allocation of Services Provided in Urban Hospitals to Rural Households*
(thousands)

Health system and service	Services received by rural households[a] minus services provided by rural institutions[b]	Large cities		
		Services provided (1)	Allocated to rural households (2)	(2)/(1)
National Health System				
Outpatient visits	1,106	—	—	—
Deliveries	74	78	25	0.32
Operations	24	—	—	—
Inpatient days	2,569	—	—	—
Social Security System				
Outpatient visits	204	—	—	—
Deliveries	9	47	5	0.11

a. Figures taken from 1974 sample survey.
b. Figures taken from COLDATOS report.

supply of that region, since the total urban excess supply is not necessarily equal to the total rural excess demand. The figures in Table 4.8 suggest that more than half the services provided in small towns by the National Health System are consumed by rural households. For inpatient care, this is also true for institutions located in intermediate cities.

Using the information in Table 4.8, the subsidies to health institutions shown in Table 4.6 can be translated into subsidies received by households, classified by location. The results are shown in Table 4.9.

Consumption of services by income groups

Tables 4.10 and 4.11 present the distribution of consumption according to income quintiles derived from the 1974 sample survey.[5] Income quintiles are again defined according to the country distribution of income.

5. The absolute consumption figures are shown in the statistical appendix, Tables SA-23 and SA-24.

Intermediate cities			Small towns		
Services provided (1)	Allocated to rural households (2)	(2)/(1)	Services provided (1)	Allocated to rural households (2)	(2)/(1)
—	—	—	1,942	1,106	0.57
55	19	0.34	60	30	0.50
63	4	0.06	31	20	0.64
2,189	1,154	0.53	2,075	1,415	0.68
—	—	—	884	204	0.23
20	4	0.20	—	—	—

Table 4.9. *Health Subsidies Received by Households, Classified by Location of Household, 1974*
(millions of pesos)

Institution and service	Location of household					
	Large cities	Inter-mediate cities	Small towns	Urban total	Rural areas	Country total
National Health System						
Hospitals						
Outpatient visits	29.2	26.5	28.4	84.1	40.0	124.1
Deliveries	1.5	1.3	1.2	4.0	2.6	6.6
Operations	90.1	51.1	11.2	152.4	23.9	176.3
Inpatient days	162.0	120.6	90.3	372.9	338.5	711.4
Health centers	107.6	61.8	89.3	258.7	79.8	338.5
Social Security System						
Hospitals						
Outpatient visits	241.3	101.2	29.3	371.8	16.7	388.5
Deliveries	2.6	0.8	0.4	3.8	0.6	4.4
Operations	120.6	26.5	12.5	159.6	1.0	160.6
Inpatient days	247.8	75.3	29.9	353.0	12.7	365.7

Table 4.10. *Services Provided*
by National Health System Hospitals and Health Centers,
Classified by Location of Household
(percentage distribution reported by households in the 1974 sample survey)

	Location of household					
Income quintile (*poorest to richest*)	*Large cities*	*Inter-mediate cities*	*Small towns*	*Urban average*	*Rural areas*	*Country average*
Hospitals						
Outpatient visits						
1	16.4	12.4	33.2	20.5	26.5	22.2
2	14.6	17.6	22.8	18.4	27.6	21.1
3	18.4	17.1	26.6	20.6	22.2	21.1
4	31.5	31.0	12.4	25.0	18.8	23.2
5	19.1	21.9	5.0	15.5	4.9	12.4
Deliveries						
1	26.5	22.2	36.7	28.0	31.6	29.5
2	23.5	25.0	23.3	24.0	31.6	27.3
3	17.6	19.4	20.0	19.0	21.0	19.9
4	23.5	22.3	6.7	18.0	10.5	14.8
5	8.9	11.1	13.3	11.0	5.3	8.5
Operations						
1	24.5	12.5	36.4	22.6	40.0	26.6
2	6.1	16.7	18.2	10.7	32.0	15.6
3	8.2	33.3	—	14.3	12.0	13.8
4	24.5	25.0	27.3	25.0	16.0	22.9
5	36.7	12.5	18.1	27.4	—	21.1
Inpatient days						
1	46.1	27.0	29.4	42.1	23.2	33.7
2	14.4	23.3	23.5	13.6	31.5	21.6
3	15.7	14.5	13.9	15.0	26.8	20.2
4	9.0	25.9	13.2	15.3	14.8	15.1
5	14.8	9.3	20.0	14.0	3.7	9.4
Health centers						
Visits to nurses						
1	14.5	19.7	37.7	22.7	30.5	25.2
2	27.8	28.7	30.0	28.7	27.9	28.4
3	29.2	18.4	16.2	22.5	25.3	23.3
4	18.6	23.3	8.1	16.7	11.8	15.2
5	9.9	9.9	8.0	9.4	4.5	7.9

Table 4.11. *Services Provided by Social Security System Hospitals* (ICSS *and Cajas*), *Classified by Location of Household*
(percentage distribution reported by households in the 1974 sample survey)

Income quintile (poorest to richest)	Location of household					
	Large cities	Inter- mediate cities	Small towns	Urban average	Rural areas	Country average
Outpatient visits						
1	2.2	7.4	6.8	4.7	18.9	5.7
2	12.1	14.4	35.5	16.1	24.8	16.7
3	24.8	18.0	21.2	21.8	29.4	22.3
4	27.7	30.5	24.8	28.4	23.1	28.0
5	33.2	29.7	11.7	29.0	3.8	27.3
Deliveries						
1	—	12.4	—	4.3	33.3	9.1
2	13.7	6.3	25.0	13.0	11.2	12.7
3	40.9	6.3	37.5	28.3	22.2	27.3
4	22.7	37.5	25.0	28.3	33.3	29.1
5	22.7	37.5	12.5	26.1	—	21.8
Operations						
1	12.5	20.0	—	13.6	—	13.6
2	18.9	—	—	13.6	—	13.6
3	37.3	20.0	100.0	36.5	—	36.5
4	6.3	40.0	—	13.6	—	13.6
5	25.0	20.0	—	22.7	—	22.7
Inpatient days						
1	7.1	4.3	38.0	9.0	—	9.0
2	16.4	5.0	29.0	14.8	—	14.8
3	40.6	8.6	20.0	31.1	—	31.1
4	18.3	60.7	13.0	28.1	—	28.1
5	17.6	21.4	—	17.0	—	17.0

As shown in Table 4.9, inpatient care accounts for most of the subsidy to the National Health Service; thus the distribution of consumption of this service determines the distributive content of the subsidy. Lower-income quintiles consume the largest share of this service, and the share declines monotonically for higher-income groups. In the case of outpatient visits, the share of services consumed is similar for each of the first four quintiles, diminishing

Table 4.12. *Households Affiliated with the Social Security System,*
Classified by Income Quintile
(percentage)

Income quintile (poorest to richest)	Location of household				
	Large cities	Inter-mediate cities	Small towns	Rural areas	Country average
1	5.1	6.2	12.1	19.5	8.5
	(4.6)	(6.6)	(14.1)	(27.4)	(6.7)
2	13.1	13.8	27.4	26.3	17.1
	(14.4)	(15.9)	(21.7)	(21.2)	(16.1)
3	17.9	20.0	23.3	28.0	20.7
	(18.6)	(21.9)	(25.9)	(26.8)	(20.7)
4	25.8	26.2	21.1	18.6	24.3
	(25.8)	(25.9)	(22.1)	(17.3)	(25.2)
5	38.1	33.8	16.1	7.6	29.4
	(36.6)	(29.7)	(16.2)	(6.8)	(31.3)

Note: The distribution of individuals is given in parentheses.

sharply for the richest quintile. For surgical operations, the shares
of consumption appear more erratic across income groups.

In the Social Security System (ICSS and Cajas), 82 percent of
the subsidy is accounted for by outpatient visits and inpatient
care. The country total figures in Table 4.11 show that the three
richest quintiles have the highest shares of consumption, particularly in the case of outpatient care. For inpatient care, the shares
of consumption are concentrated in the third and fourth quintiles.

The plausibility of the figures derived for the Social Security
System can be checked by comparing them with the distribution of
households or individuals (where individuals include workers plus
their family) affiliated with this system. This distribution is shown
in Table 4.12. The distribution of affiliated individuals resembles
the distribution of outpatient visits more than it does the distribution of inpatient days, particularly in the richest quintile; the
resemblance still holds when the comparison is made at the level
of regional breakdown.

Using the figures in Tables 4.10 and 4.11 and the subsidy figures
in Table 4.9, it is possible to allocate the total health subsidy

across income quintiles and location of households.[6] The resulting subsidy per household is presented in Table 4.13. It is computed by dividing the total subsidy (allocated to each type of institution) by the total number of households in the corresponding quintile and location. Thus, the subsidy per household must be interpreted as the subsidy received by the representative family in that location and income quintile. The total subsidy per household is equal to the sum of subsidies received by the representative household from all types of institutions.

Several conclusions can be drawn from the results in Table 4.13.

(a) There is a strong difference in the subsidy for urban and rural households in the same quintile. Urban households receive a subsidy at least twice as large as that received by their rural counterparts; it is almost three times as large in the poorest quintile.

(b) In a given quintile, the subsidy tends to be larger for households living in larger cities.

(c) The subsidy is largest for the first four quintiles. Within these quintiles the highest variation is found in large cities; this variance is dominated by the large National Health System subsidy in the first quintile and the large Social Security System subsidy in the third.

An alternative way of presenting the subsidy per household is to compute, for each cell, a subsidy per household affiliated with the Social Security System and a subsidy per household not affiliated with the system. This allows identification of the intracell differences in the subsidy that are induced by affiliation with the Social Security System. Table 4.14 presents these results. The average value for the country shows the subsidy for an affiliated household (AF) as 2.4 times the one for a nonaffiliated household (NAF). The mean is much closer to the second figure, because only 22.2 percent of heads of household are affiliated with the system.[7]

---

6. See the statistical appendix, Table SA-25.

7. Households affiliated with the Social Security System, as a percentage of the households in each quintile, are, respectively:

Quintile (poorest to richest)	1	2	3	4	5	Average
Percentage of households	9.4	18.4	24.7	27.0	33.0	22.2

Table 4.13. *Health Subsidy per Household, 1974*
(pesos)

Income quintile (poorest to richest)	Location of household											
	Large cities				Intermediate cities				Small towns			
	NHS	SSS	HC	Total	NHS	SSS	HC	Total	NHS	SSS	HC	Total
1	1,085	404	166	1,655	546	206	156	908	246	82	205	533
2	245	683	220	1,148	412	183	176	771	216	138	193	547
3	213	1,141	173	1,527	345	263	100	708	198	242	141	581
4	189	491	82	762	326	543	89	958	198	119	76	393
5	162	399	27	588	134	294	35	462	368	58	122	548
Country average	271	587	103	961	317	323	98	738	235	129	160	524

Note: NHS = National Health Service hospital; SSS = Social Security System hospital; and HC = health center.

Table 4.14. *Health Subsidy per Household,*
Classified by Affiliation (AF) *and Nonaffiliation* (NAF)
with the Social Security System, 1974
(pesos)

Income quintile (poorest to richest)	Location of household								
	Large cities			Intermediate cities			Small towns		
	AF	NAF	Mean	AF	NAF	Mean	AF	NAF	Mean
1	2,062	1,556	1,655	1,221	845	908	1,089	488	533
2	1,963	714	1,148	632	828	771	671	515	547
3	3,153	605	1,527	715	704	708	1,084	436	581
4	1,325	430	762	1,514	647	958	499	359	393
5	1,118	295	588	724	283	462	205	681	548
Country average	1,697	572	961	954	627	738	701	483	524

Sensitivity analysis

To evaluate the sensitivity of the results, an alternative distribution of the subsidy was used for both the National Health System and Social Security System networks.[8] The total subsidy

---

8. The alternate distribution of public subsidies to hospitals is given in the statistical appendix, Table SA-26.

				Location of household							
Urban average				*Rural areas*				*Country average*			
NHS	SSS	HC	*Total*	NHS	SSS	HC	*Total*	NHS	SSS	HC	*Total*
551	201	183	935	259	17	63	339	395	103	119	617
279	347	198	824	341	23	60	424	310	186	130	626
247	657	144	1,048	331	27	65	423	284	381	109	774
235	438	83	756	285	28	43	356	250	314	71	635
173	337	38	548	159	14	39	212	172	295	38	505
275	398	116	789	295	23	58	376	282	255	94	631

			Location of household					
Urban average			*Rural areas*			*Country average*		
AF	NAF	*Mean*	AF	NAF	*Mean*	AF	NAF	*Mean*
1,534	844	935	286	343	339	1,096	568	617
1,236	664	824	264	439	424	1,008	539	626
2,009	581	1,048	248	445	423	1,535	523	774
1,274	484	756	270	366	356	1,159	440	635
925	333	548	132	222	212	887	315	505
1,309	561	789	254	387	376	1,148	484	631

to the former was allocated across income quintiles according to the distribution of outpatient visits by income groups; this distribution is different from the one for inpatient days, which was the main determinant of the earlier estimate of the distribution of the subsidy. The total subsidy to the sss was allocated according to the income distribution of those individuals (not households) affiliated with the system, as shown in parentheses in Table 4.12. The subsidy per household derived from this distribution is shown

Table 4.15. *Health Subsidy per Household: Summary*
(pesos)

Income quintile (poorest to richest)	Location of household					
	Large cities	Inter-mediate cities	Small towns	Urban average	Rural area	Country average
1	1,655	908	533	935	339	617
	(959)	(645)	(533)	(678)	(364)	(500)
2	1,148	771	547	824	424	626
	(1,172)	(844)	(520)	(843)	(380)	(613)
3	1,527	708	581	1,048	423	774
	(1,090)	(790)	(661)	(893)	(381)	(668)
4	762	958	393	756	356	635
	(1,091)	(800)	(417)	(871)	(419)	(734)
5	588	462	548	548	212	505
	(745)	(628)	(430)	(683)	(278)	(630)
Country average	961	738	524	789	376	631
	(961)	(738)	(524)	(789)	(376)	(631)

Note: The figures in parentheses were obtained by the alternate distribution.

in parentheses in Table 4.15, together with the subsidy figures estimated earlier.

Table 4.15 shows that at the country level the results are not particularly sensitive to this alternative method of allocating the subsidy. A change of about 20 percent is observed in the poorest and richest quintiles: the former having a lower subsidy with the alternate distribution and the latter a higher subsidy. The major difference is observed for households in large and intermediate cities in the poorest-income quintile, where the subsidy under the alternate distribution is, respectively, approximately 0.57 and 0.71 times the earlier estimate. The source of the difference is the allocation of the subsidy to the National Health System according to outpatient visits instead of inpatient days. In the poorest quintile the share for inpatient days is twice the share for outpatient visits.

The final conclusion is that despite the method of allocation used, the subsidy for each household is largest for the middle-income quintiles—the third and fourth with the alternate method —and declines to each end of the income distribution. The subsidy to the middle-income households is approximately 25 to 50 percent larger than the subsidies to the poorest and richest quintiles.

Explanatory Variables
behind the Demand for Medical Services

The data derived from the 1974 sample survey indicate that even in low-income households, private medicine represents a substantial share of the total consumption of health services. Visits to physicians in private practice account for more than half the total visits for both urban and rural regions, even in the poorest quintile. This suggests that an important fraction of the consumption of health services, even in low-income groups, takes place outside the National Health System and Social Security System.

Table 4.16 shows visits to physicians per household and per person by income group and location. The number of visits per household tends to increase with the per capita income of the family; the positive relation appears even stronger when the visits are calculated for individuals, except for rural households in the richest quintile. The data show a strong disparity between urban and rural households belonging to the same quintile; the figure for urban households is almost twice as large, even when visits to nurses are included in the rural figure.

Definition of explanatory variables

To explain this disparity, it is necessary to identify possible factors influencing households' demand for medical services. The quantity demanded is defined as the number of visits to doctors by all members of the household during 1974. Multiple regression experiments were undertaken for three definitions of the dependent variable: V_1, the number of visits to doctors in Social Security System hospitals by households affiliated with the system; V_2, the number of visits to doctors in private practice by all types of households; and V_3, the number of visits to all types of doctors by all types of households. V_3 includes V_1 and V_2 plus all the visits to doctors in institutions belonging to the National Health System.

Table 4.16. *Average Annual Visits to Physicians,*
per Household and per Person, 1974

Income quintile (poorest to richest)	Urban areas				Total per person
	per household				
	Hospitals, NHS	Hospitals, SSS	Private practice	Total	
1	1.74	0.43	2.26	4.43	0.66
2	1.40	1.31	2.45	5.16	0.86
3	1.49	1.67	2.97	6.13	1.10
4	1.44	1.73	3.81	6.98	1.40
5	0.72	1.42	4.39	6.53	1.49
Country average	1.29	1.37	3.36	6.02	1.11

It can be hypothesized that the demand for medical services will be influenced by the purchasing power of the family, to the extent that some cost is involved in obtaining the services; by the size and age composition of the family; and by variables influencing the preference of households for consuming the services.

Table 4.17 shows regression coefficients for explanatory variables used as substitutes for these causal factors. The variables used were: PERCAP, per capita income of the household; NPER, number of persons in the household; EDUC HEAD, years of schooling of head of household; EDUC WIFE, years of schooling of wife; and SHARE CHILD, number of children in a particular age bracket, as a fraction of NPER.

Regression coefficient results

The figures in Table 4.17 are regression coefficient results for urban households only; no significant results were obtained for rural households. For urban households, only V_2 and V_3 yielded significant results; V_1, visits to Social Security System doctors, did not appear to be associated with the variables described above.

V_2, visits to doctors in private practice, was the only component of the total demand for medical services responding to the hypothesized causal variables. Because these visits account for more than

| | Rural areas | | | | |
| | per household | | | | |
Hospitals, NHS	Hospitals, SSS	Private practice	Visits to nurses and health centers	Total	Total per person
0.83	0.11	1.41	0.34	2.69	0.38
0.90	0.16	1.56	0.17	2.79	0.47
0.86	0.22	1.24	0.39	2.71	0.53
1.04	0.25	2.07	0.21	3.57	0.80
0.64	0.10	1.35	0.18	2.27	0.67
0.87	0.17	1.51	0.27	2.82	0.51

half the total visits, the regressions for V_3 are dominated by the behavior of V_2.[9]

The regression results in Table 4.17 have a low R^2: only 6 to 8 percent of the observed variance is accounted for. Nevertheless, some variables appear significant, and this at least suggests new research.

Per capita income and the education variables appear significant. The elasticity with respect to income is larger for V_3: that is, the income elasticity of demand for doctors in private practice is larger than it is for doctors in public institutions. Education of the head of household has a significantly larger coefficient (almost three times as large) than education of the wife.

The elasticities for NPER are substantially lower than 1, the elasticity for V_2 being a third of that for V_3. Elasticities smaller than 1 indicate some economies of scale in the use of medical services with larger household size, this being more important for V_2.

Other demographic variables, such as the shares of children below age 18, have negative coefficients, but not all are statisti-

9. Visits to doctors in private practice represent 51 percent of the total visits for urban households in the poorest quintile and 67 percent for the ones in the richest quintile (see Table 4.16).

Table 4.17. *Regression Coefficient Results*
from Regressing the Number of Visits to Doctors as a Function
of Socioeconomic Variables of Households in Urban Areas

Independent variable	Dependent variable	
	Log of number of visits to doctors in private practice, log V_2	Log of number of visits to all doctors, log V_3
Constant	−0.278[b]	0.004
	(2.30)	(0.03)
log PERCAP	0.073[a]	0.047[a]
	(4.37)	(2.57)
log NPER	0.135[a]	0.378[a]
	(2.58)	(6.59)
log EDUC HEAD	0.171	0.182[a]
	(5.61)	(5.49)
log EDUC WIFE	0.058[b]	0.077[a]
	(2.17)	(2.63)
log SHARE CHILD (ages 0–6)	−0.047	−0.088
	(1.59)	(2.72)
log SHARE CHILD (ages 7–12)	−0.012	0.022
	(0.36)	(0.61)
log SHARE CHILD (ages 13–18)	−0.065[b]	−0.010
	(2.08)	(0.29)
	$R^2 = 0.06$	$R^2 = 0.08$
	$F = 22.6$	$F = 30.6$

Note: Values in parentheses are *t*-ratios.
a. Values significant at 1 percent in a two-tail test.
b. Values significant at 5 percent in a two-tail test.

cally significant. This implies a more intensive use of medical services by adults than by children under 18.

Appendix. A Framework for Analyzing the Incidence of the Financing of the Social Security System

Equilibrium in the labor market without the system

Assume that the supply, L^s, and demand for labor, L^d, can be written as a constant elasticity function of the wage rate:

(1) $$L^s = aW^\alpha$$

(2) $$L^d = bW^{-\beta}.$$

In equilibrium $L^s = L^d$, and:

(3)
$$\bar{W}_0 = \left(\frac{b}{a}\right)^{\frac{1}{\alpha+\beta}}$$

where $\bar{W}_0$ is the presystem equilibrium wage rate. $\bar{W}_0$ is the wage paid by employers as well as the one received by workers.

New equilibrium when implementing the system

Assume that each worker values the services provided by the system in an amount V per year. Assume furthermore that such value is proportional to the supply price W defined earlier. Denoting as $\phi/(1 + \phi)$ that factor of proportionality;

(4)
$$V = \frac{\phi}{1 + \phi}\, W.$$

The new supply price of labor now becomes:

(5)
$$W_v = W - V = W\left(\frac{1}{1 + \phi}\right).$$

If labor contributes to the system a fraction t_w of its (gross) wage, the new (or gross) supply price faced by employers becomes W_1, namely:

(6)
$$W_1 = \frac{W_v}{(1 - t_w)} = W\,\frac{1}{(1 - t_w)(1 + \phi)}.$$

Solving for W out of Equation (1) and substituting into Equation (6) gives:

(7)
$$W_1 = \frac{1}{(1 - t_w)(1 + \phi)}\left(\frac{L^s}{a}\right)^{1/\alpha}.$$

If employers also contribute a tax of t_ϵ on the wage paid, the new demand price for labor faced by workers becomes:

(8)
$$W_1 = \frac{W}{1 + t_\epsilon}.$$

Solving for W out of Equation (2) and substituting into Equation (8):

(9)
$$W_1 = \frac{1}{(1 + t_\epsilon)}\left(\frac{L^d}{b}\right)^{-1/\beta}.$$

Solving for L^s and L^d from Equations (7) and (9) and making $L^s = L^d$, the new equilibrium wage $\bar{W}_1$ is defined as a function of the presystem wage $\bar{W}_0$:

$$(10) \qquad \bar{W}_1 = \bar{W}_0 \frac{(1 + t_e)^{-\beta/k}}{(1 - t_w)^{\alpha/k} (1 + \phi)^{\alpha/k}}$$

where $\alpha + \beta = k$.

Of interest is the change in the net money wage received by labor as a fraction of the total contributions to the system per employed worker. Denoting that contribution as R:

$$(11) \qquad R = (t_w + t_e) W_1.$$

The change in the net wage as a fraction of R becomes:

$$(12) \quad \frac{\Delta}{R} = \frac{(1 - t_w) W_1 - W_0}{(t_w + t_e) W_1} = \frac{1}{(t_w + t_e)} \left[(1 - t_w) - \frac{W_0}{W_1} \right].$$

Substituting $\left(\dfrac{\bar{W}_0}{\bar{W}_1} \right)$ from Equation (10) into Equation (12) produces:

$$(13) \quad \frac{\Delta}{R} = \frac{(1 - t_w) - (1 - t_w)^{\alpha/k} (1 + \phi)^{\alpha/k} (1 + t_e)^{\beta/k}}{(t_w + t_e)}.$$

The value of ϕ

Assume that the value of V can be related to the value of R, the total contributions to the system per employed worker. If the valuation of the services of the system V is a fraction μ of the contribution R:

$$(14) \qquad V = \mu R = \mu(t_w + t_e) W_1.$$

From Equations (4) and (5):

$$(15) \qquad V = \phi W_v.$$

Substituting Equation (15) into Equation (14) and solving for ϕ:

$$(16) \qquad \phi = \frac{\mu (t_w + t_e)}{(1 - t_w)}.$$

Substituting Equation (16) into Equation (13) yields:

(17) $\dfrac{\Delta}{R}$

$$= \frac{(1 - t_w) - [(1 + \mu t_\epsilon) + t_w (\mu - 1)]^{\frac{1}{1 + (\beta / \alpha)}} (1 + t_\epsilon)^{\frac{1}{(\alpha / \beta) + 1}}}{(t_w + t_\epsilon)}$$

The fraction Δ/R shows the fraction of the financing of the system that is borne by labor. If the fraction equals 1, all the financing of the system is borne by labor; if it equals zero, all the financing is borne by employers.

Special cases

Some results for Δ/R under extreme values of the parameters are presented here.

CASE WHEN $\mu = 0$. The expression collapses into:

(18) $$\frac{\Delta}{R} = \frac{(1 - t_w) - (1 - t_w)^{\frac{1}{1 + (\beta / \alpha)}} (1 + t_\epsilon)^{\frac{1}{(\alpha / \beta) + 1}}}{(t_w + t_\epsilon)} .$$

If the supply of labor is perfectly elastic, $\alpha = \infty$, then:

(19) $$\frac{\Delta}{R} = \frac{(1 - t_w) - (1 - t_w)}{(t_w + t_\epsilon)} = 0,$$

and all the financing is borne by employers. If $\alpha = 0$, then Equation (8) can be rewritten:

(20) $$\frac{\Delta}{R} = \frac{(1 - t_w) - (1 + t_\epsilon)}{(t_w + t_\epsilon)} = -1,$$

and all the financing is borne by labor. The more inelastic the supply in relation to the demand for labor, the higher the incidence borne by labor.

CASE WHEN $\mu = 1$. In this case Equation (17) collapses into:

(21) $$\frac{\Delta}{R} = \frac{(1 - t_w) - (1 + t_\epsilon)}{(t_w + t_\epsilon)} = -1.$$

Table 4.18. *Values of* Δ/R ($t_w = 0.035$; $t_\epsilon = 0.070$)

μ	α/β					
	∞	*10*	*5*	*3*	*2*	*1*
1.0	−1.00	−1.00	−1.00	−1.00	−1.00	−1.00
0.5	−0.50	−0.54	−0.58	−0.62	−0.66	−0.75
0.25	−0.25	−0.31	−0.37	−0.43	−0.49	−0.62
0.10	−0.10	−0.18	−0.25	−0.32	−0.39	−0.54
0	0	−0.08	−0.16	−0.24	−0.32	−0.49

In other words, if employees value the services of the system in an amount equal to R, the incidence of the financing is borne completely by labor and independently of the values of α and β.

POSSIBLE VALUES RELEVANT FOR COLOMBIA. Workers affiliated with ICSS make a legal contribution to the system of approximately 3.5 percent of their gross wage. The contribution of employers is approximately twice as much—7 percent of the wage paid to employees. Table 4.18 provides values for Δ/R for alternative values of α/β and μ.

The legal incidence, $t_w/(t_w + t_\epsilon) = 0.33$, will be larger than the real incidence for values of μ below 0.25 and for ratios α/β larger than 2. A value of μ between 0.25 and 0.5 and a range of α/β between 2 and 5 yield a range of Δ/R between −0.37 and −0.66. A value of −0.50 will be used.

Chapter 5

The Distribution of Consumption
of Public Utility Services:
Electricity, Piped Water,
and Sewerage

THE SUBSIDY RECEIVED by households from consuming electricity, water, and sewerage services is not derived here. As mentioned in Chapter 1, this would require an estimate of the long-run marginal cost of providing the services in different regions. Such an estimate can be derived only from micro-studies of the cost of expanding the system of supply of these services in different regions of the country.

This chapter addresses a different set of issues concerning the distributive direction of consumption across income groups, using information from the 1974 sample survey. The first section analyzes the distributive direction of investment in these sectors between 1970 and 1974; then it discusses the availability of services in 1970 and in 1974 and the association between availability, income, and region. The second section deals specifically with the availability of services in urban areas. It attempts to identify the factors determining the probability of having the service and the probability of obtaining the service in a certain time period. The third section addresses similar questions for households located in the rural areas of the country. Some earlier estimates of the redistribution of transfers across consumers resulting from the system of tariffs in these sectors are reviewed in the appendix to this chapter.

Investment and the Availability of Services

Investment in electricity (generation and transmission) between 1970 and 1974 fluctuated between 4.5 and 7.6 percent of total government expenditure, the higher figure corresponding to 1974. In the same period investment in piped water and sewerage fluctuated between 1.7 and 2.7 percent of total government expenditure, the figure for 1974 amounting to 2.5 percent. For 1974 the total investment in these sectors represented 10.1 percent of all government expenditure. What was the distributive direction of this investment? An approximate answer can be obtained by looking at the distribution of the households that received these services during this period.

Distributive direction of investment, 1970 to 1974

Table 5.1 presents data from the 1974 sample survey on the distribution of households that reported having received these services between 1970 and 1974. Because of the sample size, results are given for the total country, not for regions.

The results show that between 45 and 55 percent of the households that received the services belong to the poorest 40 percent of households and that between 72 and 82 percent belong to the poorest 60 percent. Many of these households are in rural areas: 58.6 percent of those receiving piped water and 49.6 percent of those receiving electricity.

The large share of rural households among those which received piped water seems surprising, given the nature of the service. It might be explained by the existence of small towns in rural areas,[1] or it may result from the way availability was defined in the questionnaire. Availability of piped water was defined as a situation in which the dwelling is connected to an aqueduct or to a primary network of piped water. In rural areas, therefore, it would include all households with any type of access to an open aqueduct.

A rough estimate of the implicit mean cost of connection can be made by comparing the absolute increase in connected households

---

1. Rural areas include towns of fewer than 1,500 inhabitants.

Table 5.1. *Distribution of Households That Obtained Public Utility Services between 1970 and 1974*
(percentage)

Income quintile (poorest to richest)	Electricity	Piped water	Sewerage	Street lighting
1	26.0	31.4	24.5	25.6
2	25.1	23.6	21.3	24.4
3	25.6	26.8	29.1	22.5
4	12.0	12.6	12.0	11.9
5	11.3	5.6	13.1	15.6
Percentage of households in rural areas	49.6	58.6	18.3	0.0

(estimated by expanding the survey results) with investment between 1970 and 1974. Given the lumpy nature of investment in these sectors, however, it is difficult directly to associate the aggregate investment figures with the increase in the number of beneficiaries over so brief a period. To correct partially for this in the case of electricity, only investment in subtransmission and distribution is included—the assumption being that this component of investment is more closely associated to yearly increases in the number of beneficiaries than other components of investment.

Tables 5.2 and 5.3 show data on investment between 1970 and 1974. The total figure for the four-year period was computed by including all of the figures for 1971, 1972, and 1973 and half of the figures for 1970 and 1974. The last column presents these figures in 1974 prices: 2,866 million pesos for electricity (subtransmission and distribution) and 6,022 million pesos for water and sewerage.

By dividing the investment figures by the number of households connected in the period, the mean investment per household can be computed. The number of households connected is derived from the sample survey and also, in the case of water and sewerage, from independent official sources. These data are presented in Table 5.4.

The investment per household in water and sewerage is computed using the sample data on connected households (Estimate I) and an extreme figure from official sources (Estimate III). The official Estimate II is almost exactly equal to the sample

Table 5.2. *Investment in Electricity, 1970 to 1974*
(millions of current pesos)

Service	1970	1971	1972	1973	1974
Generation	549	1,982	1,177	2,703	3,388
Subtransmission and distribution					
Urban	295	184	250	538	714
Rural	101	63	86	185	244
Total	396	247	336	723	958
Subtransmission and distribution at 1974 prices[a]	797	445	545	998	958
Total for 1970–74	$1/2(797) + (445) + (545) + (998) + 1/2(958) = 2{,}866$				

a. The implicit price deflator of gross fixed investment was used to derive the figures in 1974 prices.
Source: Data from Departamento Nacional de Planeación, Colombia.

Table 5.3. *Investment in Piped Water and Sewerage, 1970 to 1974*
(millions of current pesos)

Institutions	1970	1971	1972	1973	1974
Public utility companies					
Bogotá, Cali, Medellín, and Barran- quilla	230	356	633	841	1,141
Other compa- nies	18	29	97	144	121
Total	248	385	730	985	1,262
INSFOPAL	198	136	198	246	243
I.N.S.	41	100	121	153	100
Total at current prices	487	621	1,049	1,384	1,605
Total at 1974 prices[a]	981	1,118	1,701	1,910	1,605
Total for 1971– 1974	$1/2(981) + (1{,}118) + (1{,}701) + (1{,}910) + 1/2(1{,}605) = 6{,}022$				

a. The implicit price deflator of gross fixed investment was used to derive the figures in 1974 prices.
Source: Data from Departamento Nacional de Planeación, Colombia.

Table 5.4. *Number of New Households Connected to the Service and Public Investment per Household between 1971 and 1974*

Service	Investment between 1970 and 1974ᵃ (millions of pesos)	Estimates of the number of new households (thousands)			Investment per household (pesos)	
		Sample	Official figuresᵇ			
		I	II	III	I	III
Piped water	} 6,022	191 } 148	212 } 152	271 } 243	40,689	24,782
Sewerage		104	91	216		
Electricity	2,866	123			23,301	

a. From Tables 5.2 and 5.3.
b. The two official estimates (II and III) are derived as follows:
Estimate II: According to INSFOPAL, 526,000 and 445,000 additional individuals in urban areas were served by piped water and sewerage, respectively, between 1970 and 1974. With an average family size of six, this implies 88,000 and 74,000 additional households, respectively. According to the sample survey, 41.4 percent of the additional households served by piped water are located in the urban area; this yields an implicit country total of 212,000 households. In the case of sewerage, the sample survey reports 81.7 percent of new households served as being in the urban area; this yields an absolute increment for the country of 91,000 households.
Estimate III: According to "El sector de Acueducto y Alcantarillados," Documento D.N.P., June 1976, approximately 2 and 1.6 million additional individuals received piped water and sewerage services, respectively, between 1970 and 1975. The number of households connected between 1970 and 1974 was estimated by multiplying these figures by 0.8 and then dividing them by 5.9, the weighted average family size of the households connected, according to the survey.

survey figure. Because investments in water and sewerage are only available as an aggregate, the estimates on investment per household are derived by using the mean figures, 148,000 and 243,000 new households, respectively, which yield mean investment figures of 24,782 and 40,689 pesos. For electricity the estimated figure is 23,301 pesos. These are country averages and do not provide separate information on investment per household in urban and rural areas. Although it is possible to obtain a breakdown of investment figures according to location, the sample of new households connected was too small to provide reliable expanded figures at the rural and urban levels.

Availability of services and its association with income and region, 1970 and 1974

Table 5.5 presents data from the sample survey on the percentage of families having services in 1974. Figures in parentheses are preliminary results from a 4 percent sample of the 1973 census of

Table 5.5 *Families with Services, 1974*
(percentage)

	Electricity	Piped water	Sewerage	Garbage collection	Street lighting
Large cities	98.9	95.1	90.9	82.4	97.3
	(93.6)	(90.0)	(86.4)		
Intermediate cities	94.3	90.1	77.2	70.3	88.9
	(86.0)	(84.7)	(69.0)		
Small towns	72.4	79.8	61.9	46.4	78.4
	(69.6)	(74.5)	(50.7)		
Rural areas	15.6	19.9	5.1	—[a]	—[a]
Country	62.7	63.2	51.3	—	—

Note: Values in parentheses are preliminary figures from a 4 percent sample of the 1973 census of population and housing.
a. Service is not available in this location.

population and housing, which was carried out about eighteen months before the sample survey.

Even the lower bound estimate of the sample survey (using a confidence interval of 95 percent) yielded a larger value than the census estimate. The difference might be explained by an increase in coverage between the times the census and the survey were made. Another and perhaps more important source of difference might lie in the reporting of illegal connections. Probably households with illegal connections were less willing to report them to census interviewers than to survey interviewers.[2]

Tables SA-27 through SA-32 in the statistical appendix show the proportion of households with services for each quintile in the regional distribution of income. The probability of having a service is clearly associated with income level and location. For a given income bracket, the proportion of households with services increases if these households are located in larger cities.

LINEAR PROBABILITY FUNCTIONS. To demonstrate the independent effect of per capita income and location, linear probability functions were estimated for 1970 and 1974. The purpose is to explain a binary dependent variable: the household either has or

---

2. This argument applies to electricity; it is harder to think of situations of illegal connection for the other services, especially sewerage.

does not have a particular public service. If individual (not grouped) data are used, the simplest technique is to use ordinary least squares, where a dependent variable y is 1 if the household has the service or 0 if it does not. The 1, 0 nature of the regressand enables the conditional expectation of y, given the vector of independent variables $\mathbf{X}$, to be interpreted as the conditional probability that the event will occur given $\mathbf{X}$, $P(\mathbf{X})$.

$$(1) \qquad E(y/\mathbf{X}) \; = \; P(\mathbf{X}) \; = \; \beta_0 \, + \, \beta_1 x_1 \, + \, \beta_2 x_2 \, \ldots$$

The approach summarized in Equation (1), the linear probability function, allows the regression coefficients to be interpreted as the marginal contribution of the respective independent variable to the probability.[3] The interpretation of these coefficients must take into account that $P(\mathbf{X})$ is not constrained to the unit interval; what becomes relevant is to what extent the range of observations whose behavior is being explained lies in the interval.

In this particular case a bivariate regression, $P_J(x)$, becomes relevant, where J refers to the region and x to the household per capita income. After several experiments, the inverse form was adopted (based on the t-ratio of the coefficient of the income variable):

$$(2) \qquad P_J \; = \; a_J \, + \, b_J \left(\frac{1}{x} \right).$$

A theoretical advantage of this function is its asymptotic property if $a \leq 1$, in other words, P has an upper bound of less than 1 when b_J has the correct (negative) sign. In this case the income elasticity of the probability becomes equal to:

$$(3) \qquad E_J \; = \; x \, \frac{dP_J}{dx} \; = \; \frac{b_J}{x} \, ,$$

where E_J is defined as the change in P when per capita income changes by 1 percent. E_J declines with income, that is, it is inversely proportional to x.

Table 5.6 presents the estimates of a_J and b_J for each region and each type of service for 1970 and 1974. Although the t-ratios

---

3. Generalized least squares estimation should be used because of heteroskedasticity: that is, the variance of the disturbance term depends on $\mathbf{X}$.

Table 5.6. *Estimated Regression Coefficients in the Linear Probability Function*

	Constant[a]				Coefficient of $(1/x)$[b]			
Service	Large cities	Inter-mediate cities	Small towns	Rural areas	Large cities	Inter-mediate cities	Small cities	Rural areas
Sewerage								
1970	0.93	0.84	0.65		−16.9	−34.4	−19.9	—[c]
					(5.3)	(5.8)	(5.1)	
1974	0.95	0.86	0.70		−15.7	−32.5	−19.6	—[c]
					(5.5)	(5.6)	(5.1)	
Piped water								
1970	0.96	0.94	0.83	0.17	−15.6	−21.4	−15.4	−8.6
					(6.0)	(4.8)	(4.5)	(4.3)
1974	0.98	0.94	0.85	0.22	−12.3	−14.1	−13.4	−6.1
					(5.8)	(3.3)	(4.2)	(2.6)
Electricity								
1970	0.98	0.96	0.79	0.12	−6.2	−16.2	−15.2	−8.8
					(3.3)	(4.3)	(4.2)	(3.0)
1974	0.99	0.98	0.81	0.21	−2.3	−13.3	−10.9	−10.6
					(2.2)	(4.1)	(3.2)	(4.9)
Street lighting								
1970	0.98	0.89	0.75		−10.9	−26.5	−16.8	—[c]
					(5.0)	(4.9)	(4.5)	
1974	0.99	0.93	0.83		−6.2	−16.8	−11.3	—[c]
					(3.9)	(3.8)	(3.9)	
Garbage collection								
1970	0.87	0.75	0.54		−21.1	−36.4	−19.9	—[c]
					(5.7)	(5.5)	(5.1)	
1974	0.87	0.80	0.58		−19.6	−39.4	−25.0	—[c]
					(5.2)	(6.2)	(6.4)	

Note: Values in parentheses show the t-ratio of the coefficient.
a. The t-ratio of the constant term is always larger than 10.
b. x measures monthly per capita household income in Colombian pesos.
c. Service is not available in this location.

are significant (sample sizes vary from 700 to 1,200 observations), the R^2 were extremely low; less than 5 percent.[4]

4. The interpretation of the correlation coefficient is ambiguous in the binary dependent variable case, particularly if the function is curvilinear. For a full treatment, see J. Netter and E. Scott Maynes, "On the Appropriateness of the Correlation Coefficient with a 0, 1 Dependent Variable," *Journal of the American Statistical Association* (June 1970).

Figure 5.1. *Probability of a Household Having Electricity, as a Function of Income*

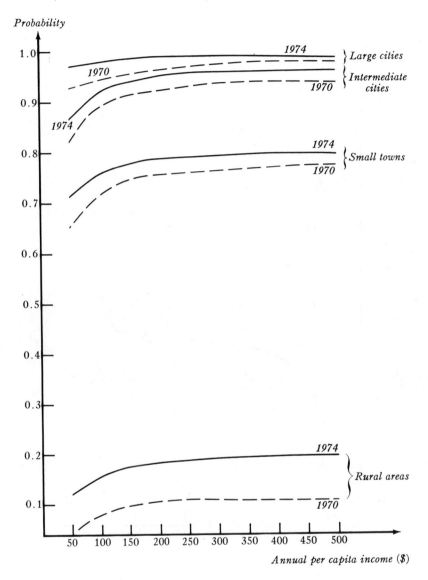

Figure 5.2. *Probability of a Household Having Sewerage, as a Function of Income*

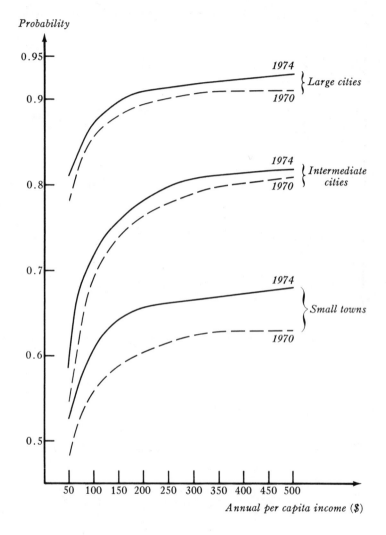

Tables SA-33 through SA-37 in the statistical appendix show estimates of *P* for alternative dollar values of annual per capita household income. In each table those values are shown for a particular service in different locations and for 1970 and 1974. They are also presented in the text in Figures 5.1 to 5.5.

Figure 5.3. *Probability of a Household Having Piped Water, as a Function of Income*

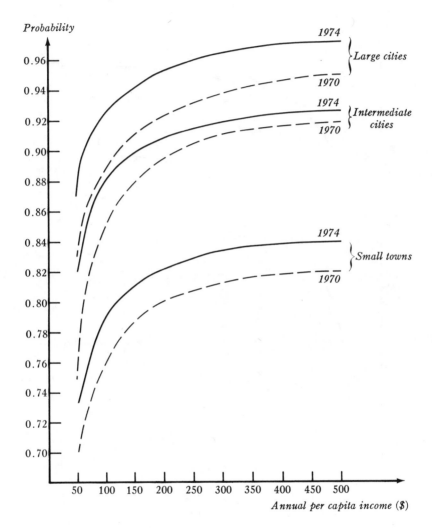

INTERPRETATION OF RESULTS. The relation between the probability and income appears stronger in intermediate cities and small towns. It shows that lower-income groups in these locations have relatively less access to services than do their counterparts in large cities. The relation appears to be weaker in the case of

Figure 5.4. *Probability of a Household Having Garbage Collection, as a Function of Income*

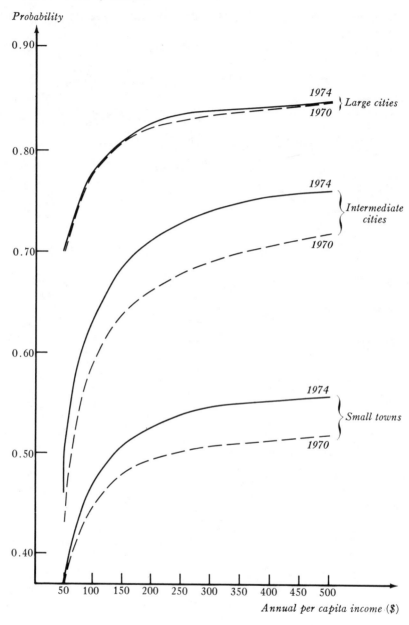

Figure 5.5. *Probability of a Household Having Street Lighting, as a Function of Income*

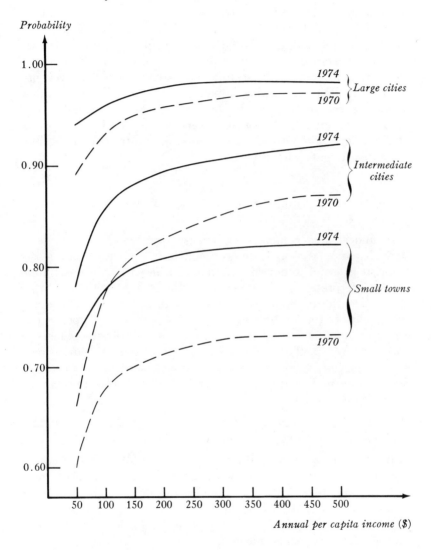

electricity, particularly in large cities. As shown in Figure 5.1, the probability of having electricity in large cities is more than 95 percent, even with a per capita income of $50 a year. (The reported mean per capita income of the poorest 10 percent of households in those cities is $59 a year.)

The weaker relation found in the case of electricity is to be expected. The possibility of illegal connection, a widespread practice in Colombia, is easier for electricity than for other services; moreover, the availability of the service or the location of the supply is usually more evenly distributed among all income levels than for the other services. Investment in transmission of electricity is cheaper than in the other sectors and usually has been given priority in public policymaking. Finally, on the demand side, income has less effect on the use of electricity when it is available at a normal connection cost. For other services, especially piped water and sewerage, the network can be used only after making a minimum investment in housing.

Public Services and Substitutes in Urban Areas

In undertaking a more comprehensive multivariate analysis of variables associated with the availability of services across households, it is useful to develop a framework in which the association can be interpreted as a cause-effect relation.

The identification of the causal variables that determine the availability of public services to households becomes important in (a) understanding the determinants of the distributive effects of those services to the extent that they provide a substantial consumer surplus in relation to alternative (nonpublic) sources of supply[5] and in (b) identifying those causal variables that can be manipulated by public policy.

Availability of services in a supply-demand context

In developing such a framework, it is useful to distinguish between the two situations in which a particular household does not consume a service: either because the supply network is geographically inaccessible (the connection cost to the family has an infinite price) or because the household could be connected at a certain cost, but decides not to do so.

---

5. Obviously a comparison between the publicly supplied service and the alternative substitute ought to be carried out in efficiency units of the service. This is particularly true when strong differences in quality exist between sources: for example, light and candlelight.

The second situation is basically determined by demand and results from a voluntary choice by the household. Because the factors determining this choice (or the variables behind the demand) may be different from the variables determining the location of the network (or the variables behind the supply), this supply-demand mechanism behind the availability of services should be recognized explicitly.

The empirical significance of situations of no consumption because of demand considerations becomes evident from the following figures for urban households:

Percentage of families without the service	*Electricity*	*Piped water*	*Sewerage*
To whom the service was offered	10	16	11
With a neighbor with service less than one block away	73	54	22

Both situations are alternative concepts of being on the supply network. The first is a more strict definition, since connection is possible only if the service is offered by the public utility company. Under the second definition, connection is possible whenever the household is less than a block from a neighbor with the service.[6] Households without services because of voluntary choice (lack of demand) represent a substantial fraction of the total families without services, particularly for electricity and piped water. Understanding what determines this choice becomes important in explaining the different availability of services across families.

REFORMULATING THE LINEAR PROBABILITY FUNCTION. Direct estimation of $P(\mathbf{X})$, the probability of having the service as a function of a vector $\mathbf{X}$, does not fully capture the supply-demand mechanism discussed above; it does not identify the extent to which a particular variable or characteristic, x_i, influences P through the demand or supply side.

For example, in the earlier results, where the availability of the service is regressed on the per capita income of the household,

---

6. When poor neighborhoods are located in parts of the city below river or sea level, sewerage connection becomes difficult; when they are located higher than reservoir altitudes, connections to the piped water system become prohibitive because water would have to be pumped. In both cases, these areas may be close to areas with services.

it is not possible to distinguish to what extent the income variable operates through supply or demand. On the one hand, the level of household income determines the behavior of the public utility companies concerning expansion of the network in particular neighborhoods. On the other hand, income affects the household's decision to get connected, however, if connection is technically possible.

The problem can be specified by considering P as the product of two independent probabilities: the probability of a household being on the supply network of the service, P^s, that is, the probability of having access to the network at the connection cost set by public utility companies, and the probability of accepting or demanding the service, P^d, if offered at this connection cost, that is, demanding the service when the household is on the supply schedule.

This specification can be written as:

$$(4) \qquad P(\mathbf{X}_1, \mathbf{X}_2) = P^s (\mathbf{X}_1) \, P^d (\mathbf{X}_2)$$

According to Equation (4) the probability of consuming the service, P, is equal to the probability of being on the supply schedule, P^s, multiplied by the probability that the household will demand the service at the cost of connection, P^d. Both P^s and P^d can be thought of as functions of vectors of variables $\mathbf{X}_1$ and $\mathbf{X}_2$, respectively, that are estimated independently. $\mathbf{X}_1$ includes variables determining the utility company's policy on locating the supply network. $\mathbf{X}_2$ measures demand-oriented variables: that is, the cost of connection relative to the income of the household and other socioeconomic characteristics of the household that govern this demand.

Possibly the vectors $\mathbf{X}_1$ and $\mathbf{X}_2$ will have common elements, that is, variables affecting both supply and demand. In this sense, supply and demand are not completely independent; if the location of expansions of supply is affected by the possibility of households getting connected, some of the variables entering P^d will also enter P^s with the same sign.

EMPIRICAL ESTIMATION. The empirical estimation of P, P^d, and P^s can be illustrated as follows. Divide the total number of households (the area of the square below) between the number of households with the service, A, the number without the service that are on the supply schedule of the service, B, and the number without service that are not on the supply schedule, C. Thus, $B + C$ is the number of households without the service.

Households with the service *(On the supply and demand)* A	
Households without the service	
(On the supply) B	*(Not on the supply)* C

	Estimation of P	Estimation of P^s	Estimation of P^d
Sample size	$A + B + C$	$A + B + C$	$A + B$
Definition of dependent variable	$\begin{cases} A_i = 1 \\ B_i = 0 \\ C_i = 0 \end{cases}$	$A_i = 1$ $B_i = 1$ $C_i = 0$	$A_i = 1$ $B_i = 0$
Mean probability	$\dfrac{A}{A + B + C}$	$\dfrac{A + B}{A + B + C}$	$\dfrac{A}{A + B}$

The probability of having the service, P, is estimated by defining a binary dependent variable, where a family with the service gets a value 1 ($A_i = 1$) and a family without the service a value 0 ($B_i = 0$, $C_i = 0$). In estimating P^s, all the families who are on the supply schedule receive the value 1 ($A_i = 1$, $B_i = 1$) and all that are not, a value of 0 ($C_i = 0$).

P^d is estimated with a subset of the households: that is, only those on the supply schedule, $A + B$. The families on the supply schedule who do demand the service receive the value 1 ($A_i = 1$); those who do not demand it receive a value 0 ($B_i = 0$). The product of the mean value for P^s and P^d yields the mean value of P.

In the above framework, the contribution of a variable x_i to the total probability P is different if traced through P^s and P^d than if it is measured by estimating P directly. Assume that the following linear probability functions for P^s and P^d are estimated:

(5) $$P^s(\mathbf{X_1}) = a_0 + a_1 x_1 + a_2 x_2 \ldots.$$

(6) $$P^d(\mathbf{X_2}) = b_0 + b_1 x_1 + b_2 x_2 \ldots.$$

The contribution to P of a variable x_i becomes, by using Equation (4), equal to:

(7)
$$\frac{\partial P}{\partial x_i} = \frac{\partial P^s}{\partial x_i} P^d (\mathbf{X}_2) + \frac{\partial P^d}{\partial x_i} P^s (\mathbf{X}_1)$$

(8)
$$\frac{\partial P}{\partial x_i} = a_i P^d (\mathbf{X}_2) + b_i P^s (\mathbf{X}_1).$$

It is clear that $\partial P/\partial x_i$ is not a constant, but is itself a function of the vectors $\mathbf{X}_2$ and $\mathbf{X}_1$.

Direct specification of P as a linear probability function of all the variables included in $\mathbf{X}_1$ and $\mathbf{X}_2$ can be shown to be inconsistent with Equations (5) and (6). For example, let P be specified as:

(9)
$$P(\mathbf{X}_1, \mathbf{X}_2) = c_0 + c_1 x_1 + c_2 x_2 \ldots$$

In this case the effect of x_i on P, namely $\partial P/\partial x_i = c_i$, is constant and independent of $\mathbf{X}_1$ and $\mathbf{X}_2$, a result contradicting Equation (8).

The contradiction results from the fact that a linear specification of P^s and P^d cannot yield a linear specification of P, a product of P^s and P^d. The correct direct specification of P is a quadratic function with interaction terms between the independent variables. From these considerations it can be concluded that it is not possible directly to compare a_i and b_i with the parameter c_i, which is obtained by direct estimation of P as a linear function.

P, P^s, and P^d will be estimated by defining a family on the supply schedule as one having a neighbor with the service at a distance of less than one block. This definition reasonably reflects a situation where households could effectively be connected if they were willing to pay the connection cost. The alternative definition, households to whom the service was formally offered, was considered too strict and limiting.

In addition to the size of city variable defined before, the following explanatory variables are included: dirt floor in the dwelling; rural migrant (households who lived in the rural area in 1970, 4 years before the interview); logarithm of the monthly per capita income of the household in pesos of November 1974; logarithm of the years of schooling completed by the head of household; logarithm of the age of the head of household; and logarithm of the numbers of years that the household has lived in the municipality.

All continuous variables are included in their logarithmic form.

This specification was usually best in terms of the t-ratios of the coefficient. The rest of the variables—city size, dirt floor, and rural migrant—are included as dummy variables.

When a continuous variable is entered in a log form in the linear probability function, its coefficient, given the 0-to-1 nature of P, can be interpreted as an elasticity. This elasticity is defined as the change in the probability when the independent variable changes by 1 percent.[7]

RESULTS FOR ELECTRICITY. Table 1.9 (in Chapter 1) shows the estimates for P, P^d, and P^s for four population groupings: total urban population, the poorest 40 and the poorest 20 percent of families according to household per capita income, and population in small towns. At the bottom of each grouping are the mean values of P, P^d, and P^s. The product of the mean values for P^d and P^s yields the mean value for P.

The size of city dummies shows that small towns have a substantially lower value of P than do the intermediate cities. This difference, however, is basically a demand effect as summarized by the coefficient of the small towns dummy in P^d. This coefficient is four times the coefficient for small towns in P^s, independent of the sample group being used. This result is of interest in the sense that the lower value of P for small towns is not associated with discrimination by the public utility companies (location of the network), but with factors behind the demand for the service.[8]

The probability of having the service is highly sensitive to the dirt-floor characteristic of the dwelling. If P^s and P^d are estimated separately, the effect is significant in both supply and demand, particularly the latter. Dirt floor is perhaps a good substitute for the permanent income of the family, a variable that would influence P^d. To find a significant and strong coefficient in P^s would mean that network location is negatively associated with that characteristic of households. It reflects a situation where network expansion by the electricity companies depends on the perceived probability of the household becoming connected and where dirt floor, as viewed by these companies, indicates this probability. It

7. If $P = \alpha_0 + \alpha_1 \log x_1 \ldots$, then $\alpha_1 = \dfrac{\partial P}{\partial \log x_1}$.

8. The interpretation rests heavily on accepting the definition of being on the supply schedule.

could also reflect such institutional constraints on the company's expansion policies as the lack of legal status of the dwelling, which is often associated with the dirt-floor variable.

Log-of-per-capita-income is significant in P and P^d for the total urban population and small towns. It is not significant when the population is stratified by income group, since it diminishes the variance of the income variable. This variable is particularly strong on the demand side in small cities; the coefficient of 0.11 means that doubling the per capita household income will increase the probability of demanding the service by 11 percentage points. It is interesting that per capita income is significant in P^d, but not in P^s, which suggests that although it influences the demand for the service, the public utility companies do not perceive it to indicate probability of connection (to the extent that probability affects the location of supply).

The rural-migrant characteristic is more statistically significant and has a stronger effect in P^d than in P^s. The effect is particularly strong within low-income groups, particularly in the poorest 20 percent of the urban population.

Log-of-schooling and log-of-age-of-head-of-household—variables that theoretically operate through demand—sometimes also appear significant on the supply side, which could reflect the impossibility of separating supply and demand, given the nature of the sample.

RESULTS FOR PIPED WATER. Table 1.10 shows that if the effect of other variables is held constant, the effect of city size becomes less important for piped water than for electricity. The difference between intermediate cities and large cities appears to be basically a supply phenomenon; the difference between large cities and small towns is basically a demand phenomenon.

The effect of dirt floor is again extremely strong and significant on both the supply and the demand sides. It presents a pattern similar to that of electricity. The rural-migrant characteristic appears to affect demand, becoming insignificant on the supply side. The income variable operates basically on the demand side, but with less strength than for electricity; the same is true for years-of-schooling-of-head-of-household. Years-in-the-same-municipality is significant on the demand side and has a negative sign. One way of interpreting this result is that the longer the household remains without the service, the lower the probability that the household will demand the service today.

RESULTS FOR SEWERAGE. Table 1.11 shows similar city size dummies for intermediate cities and small towns in the results for P. For intermediate cities it basically operates on the supply side; for small towns it operates through both demand and supply.

The dirt-floor characteristic is important, especially on the supply side; it is substantially stronger than in the case of the other two services. As expected, the income variable operates basically through demand. On the other hand, the schooling variable and the years-in-the-same-municipality variable appear more significant on the supply side; the reasons for this type of unexpected result are discussed below.

PROBLEM OF LACK OF VARIATION. The data used in the earlier analysis did not provide enough variation in the dependent variable. As suggested by the mean values, most observations had the value 1: that is, households with the service. Mean values for the total urban area are usually larger than 0.80 and were frequently larger than 0.90.

This lack of variation results from the basic objective of this study—to provide statistically significant figures for the availability of services by major breakdowns of the population. The sample survey was designed for this purpose and not to provide the degree of variation required for multivariate analysis.

The large number of households with services sampled not only affects the overall variability of the dependent variable, but also influences the possibility of separating supply and demand: that is, the factors behind P^d from the factors behind P^s.

Households with the service (A) are on the supply schedule and demand the service: that is, in estimating both P^s and P^d, they have the value 1. This common set of households is large enough to prevent the necessary variation between the data used to estimate P^d and those used to estimate P^s. Further, a large value of A makes the results very sensitive to the size of B (households without the service, but on the supply schedule) relative to C (households without the service and not on the supply schedule). The relatively small number of households without the service makes the estimates of P^s and P^d sensitive to the distribution of these households according to their position on the supply schedule.

Smaller mean values of P can increase the possibility of separating demand from supply; this is shown when the results for the total urban areas are compared with those for small towns. In small towns the fraction of households with services is substantially smaller than in the total population. The variables that might influence demand (rural-migrant, per-capita-income, and years-of-schooling) become more significant in P^d and less significant in P^s when moving from the total urban estimates to the small town estimates.

OMITTING THE COST OF CONNECTION VARIABLE. Theoretically, variations in the cost of connection should help to explain variations in P^d. The sample survey did not yield information on the connection cost actually paid by households with the service or the cost faced by a household with the possibility of getting connected.

The possibility of determining the effect of the cost of connection depends on finding enough variation in this variable across households. For urban Colombia, the cost structure for each service tends to vary across cities. Generally speaking, two cost components can be distinguished: (a) a component reflecting the direct cost of installation, that is, labor and the cost of the meter, and (b) a fee, which for water and sewerage is usually some function of the assessed value of the property and which for electricity is a function of meter capacity.[9]

What is relevant here is the extent to which the omission of the cost variable biases the coefficient of the variables that have been included: that is, the missing variable bias. This bias occurs if there is a significant association in the sample between the omitted variables and the included variables. If the coefficient of the cost variable in the demand equation is presumed to be negative, the sign of the bias will depend on the sign of the above association. If the association is positive, the estimated coefficient of the included variable will have a negative bias; if it is negative, the bias will be positive.

If the cost of connection increases with property values, it will also increase with household per capita income. This suggests a negative bias in the income coefficient estimated in the linear

---

9. For a detailed analysis of the structure of connection cost, see Johannes F. Linn, "Public Utilities in Metropolitan Bogotá: Organization, Service Levels and Financing," Urban and Regional Economics Division, Development Economics Department, (Washington, D.C.: World Bank, May 1976; processed).

probability function; the expected value of the estimate is lower than the coefficient in the true model. In other words, the estimates of the income elasticities in these functions tend to underestimate the true coefficient.

The magnitude of the bias depends not only on the magnitude of the association between the omitted and included variables, but also on the size of the coefficient of the omitted variable in the true theoretical model: that is, the size of the cost-of-connection elasticity. If this (price) elasticity is, itself, a function of per capita income, it is expected to be higher in absolute terms for lower incomes. The bias described above will differ when the sample is broken down by income groups; it will be larger for the estimates derived for lower-income quintiles.

Changes in the availability of services between 1970 and 1974

The change over time in the availability of services to different income groups can be used to indicate the distributive direction of public investment in these sectors.

SHARE TO LOW-INCOME GROUPS. The 1974 sample survey gives information on whether a particular urban household had a particular service in 1970. These data allow the computations shown in Table 5.7, where households who became connected to a particular service between 1970 and 1974 are shown according to their position in the urban income distribution. For electricity, water, and sewerage, 60, 70, and 55 percent of these households, respectively, belonged to the two lowest-income quintiles. The distributive direction of investment has been progressive in the sense that lower-income groups have had a larger share in the expansion of the total availability of these services. This comparison, however, ignores the fact that most households who did not have a service in 1970 belonged to the lower-income groups in the first place. It might well be that although investment has, in one sense, favored lower-income groups, the effect has been small relative to the potential number of beneficiaries: that is, relative to the initial number of households without the service.

Table 5.8 shows the number of households that received a service between 1970 and 1974 as a percentage of the households without a service in 1970. The results are again presented according to city size and income group in the urban income distribution.

Table 5.7. *Distribution of Urban Households That Became Connected between 1970 and 1974*

(percentage of all households with the service)

Income quintile[a] (poorest to richest)	Electricity	Piped water	Sewerage
1	31.1	34.3	27.7
2	28.4	35.4	27.5
3	9.4	11.4	13.8
4	13.5	8.8	14.9
5	17.6	10.1	16.1

a. Quintiles in the urban income distribution.

Table 5.8. *Urban Households That Became Connected between 1970 and 1974 as a Percentage of the Households without the Service in 1970, Classified by City Size and Urban Income Distribution*

Income group[a]	Large cities	Inter-mediate cities	Small towns	Urban average
Electricity				
1st quintile	61	45	12	23
2nd quintile	73	10	13	20
Upper 60 percent	47	07	14	16
Average	66	08	14	18
Piped water				
1st quintile	37	24	12	25
2nd quintile	52	32	22	34
Upper 60 percent	65	19	14	25
Average	48	27	16	27
Sewerage				
1st quintile	22	12	11	15
2nd quintile	34	16	07	18
Upper 60 percent	17	06	13	18
Average	28	14	13	17

a. Quintiles in the urban income distribution.

Table 5.9. *The Probabilities of Having Had a Service in 1970*
(P_{70}) *and of Having Obtained a Service between 1970 and 1974* (Π):
A Comparison of Regression Coefficients

Explanation variables	Electricity		Piped water		Sewerage	
	P_{70}	Π	P_{70}	Π	P_{70}	Π
Constant	0.95	0.69	0.90	0.45	0.84	0.32
	(70.6)	(5.4)	(57.7)	(8.7)	(44.8)	(9.4)
Small towns	−0.15	−0.49	−0.02	−0.33	−0.18	−0.14
	(10.2)	(6.8)	(1.7)	(3.7)	(9.1)	(3.3)
Intermediate cities	−0.02	−0.35	−0.06	−0.26	−0.11	−0.15
	(2.01)	(4.1)	(4.0)	(3.9)	(6.1)	(3.3)
Dirt floor	−0.34	−0.30	−0.34	−0.14	−0.47	−0.14
	(16.7)	(5.9)	(14.5)	(2.8)	(16.9)	(3.9)
Inverse of income	−6.1		−8.5	—	−9.9	—
	(3.9)		(4.6)		(4.5)	
Rural migrant (1970 to 1974)	—		—	0.28	—	—
				(3.6)		
Urban migrant (1970 to 1974)				0.17		
	—		—	(3.3)	—	—

Note: Values in parentheses are t-coefficients.

The last column shows that lower-income groups have benefited increasingly in relative terms from investment in electricity. This is not true in the case of sewerage or piped water. If the income bracket is held constant, the increase appears substantially larger for big cities than for intermediate cities and small towns.

MARGINAL PROBABILITY OF HAVING A SERVICE. The above considerations can be analyzed better if the probability of obtaining the service per unit of time, in this case between 1970 and 1974, is defined as an analogue to the concept of P defined earlier. Consequently, Π will be defined as the probability that a household living in the urban area in 1974, which did not have the service in 1970 (no matter where it was located), did obtain the service between 1970 and 1974.

Table 5.9 shows the estimates of the regression coefficients for Π and for P_{70}, the probability of having had the service in 1970. Per capita income was not significant in estimating Π, so it was excluded from the final equations presented in the table.

In estimating Π, the concepts of urban and rural migrants are included as dummy variables. Rural migrant is defined as any household that migrated to the urban area between 1970 and 1974; urban migrant is defined as any household that changed dwellings within the urban area during that period.

EMPIRICAL RESULTS. For electricity and piped water, the dummies for city size are substantially more negative for Π than for P_{70}, which means that being in an intermediate or small city affects negatively the probability of obtaining services over time. In other words, the negative effects have been stronger on the marginal probability (Π) than on the probability at one point in time (P_{70}).

In interpreting these phenomena it is useful to resort again to the concepts of supply and demand behind either P_{70} or Π. The negative effect could partly result from investment that benefited basically large cities, or from relatively more households moving onto the supply network of the service. Another interpretation (controlling for the other variables in the regression) is that households in large cities that were already on the supply network in 1970 had a stronger tendency to demand the service than like households in smaller cities. The size of the sample, however, did not allow testing for this particular set of hypotheses.

For piped water and sewerage, the dirt-floor dummy is less negative for Π than for P_{70}. Again, this result can be interpreted either as a demand or supply phenomenon or as a combination of the two. If this variable is an indicator of permanent income (through demand), it suggests that at the margin, the probability of demanding the service becomes less sensitive to income. If dirt floor determines a company's decisions on network location, it would mean that at the margin, dirt floor has had a lower influence on new expansions of the network in particular neighborhoods.

Perhaps the most interesting results for Π are the large positive coefficients found for migrants in the case of piped water. The results mean that the probability of having obtained the service in the urban area between 1970 and 1974 is larger for households that migrated during that period from rural areas (28 percentage points more than those that did not change their residence), as well as for those that changed residence within the urban areas during that period (17 percentage points more than those that did not change their residence).

One explanation for this result could be that migrants are more "public service achievers" than nonmigrants are—achievement being expressed in their desire for dwellings with piped water. This is particularly true if the availability of piped water is one reason for rural-to-urban or any intra-urban migration. The fact that this is true only for piped water suggests that the availability of water is a more important reason for migration than the availability of the other services.

Earlier, when estimating P for water in 1974, the rural-migrant characteristic had a significant negative coefficient, -0.07 (see Table 1.10). How can this result be reconciled with the positive coefficient found in the estimation of Π?

The value of P for 1974 can be thought of as the weighted average of P for 1974 for nonmigrants, P_{74}^{NM} (that is, households that already were living in the urban area in 1970), and the probability that migrants from rural areas between 1970 and 1974 obtained the service on moving to the urban area, Π^M. The weights are the share of the two groups in the number of households in urban areas in 1974.[10] A higher fraction of rural migrants would affect negatively the value of P for 1974 if $P_{74}^{NM} > \Pi^M$. This result, however, is perfectly consistent with $\Pi^M > \Pi^{NM}$, that is, the probability of a migrant obtaining the service during a period, in this case 1970 to 1974, is larger than for a nonmigrant.[11]

---

10. A distinction should be made between the probability of obtaining the service in the urban area for a migrant household that did and one that did not have the service before migrating. Given the sample size, it was not possible to test for such a difference. The implicit assumption is either that both probabilities are similar or that the fraction of migrant households that did have piped water in the rural area was negligible.

11. Denote P_{74} as:

(1′) $$P_{74} = [1 - (M/T)]\, P_{74}^{NM} + (M/T)\, \Pi^M,$$

where (M/T) indicates the share of rural migrants between 1970 and 1974 as a fraction of total households in urban areas in 1974. A negative effect of (M/T) on P_{74} can be defined as:

(2′) $$\partial P_{74}/\partial(M/T) = -P_{74}^{NM} + \Pi^M < 0$$

or

(3′) $$P_{74}^{NM} > \Pi^M.$$

Denoting P_{74}^{NM} as:

(4′) $$P_{74}^{NM} = P_{70}^{NM} + (1 - P_{70}^{NM})\, \Pi^{NM} = P_{70}^{NM}(1 - \Pi^{NM}) + \Pi^{NM}.$$

Substituting Equation (4′) into Equation (3′), the latter can be rewritten as:

(5′) $$P_{70}^{NM} > (\Pi^M - \Pi^{NM})/(1 - \Pi^{NM}).$$

The result, $\Pi^M > \Pi^{NM}$, found in the estimates of Π presented earlier, is consistent with Equation (2′) if P_{70}^{NM} is large enough to fulfill the condition (5′).

Urban households without services

For future investment policy, it is useful to identify the location of households without services in relation to the location of the supply network. The higher the percentage of households that are relatively near the network, the smaller the marginal investment required to provide them with the service. The more households who do not have a service because of demand factors, the more important are demand-oriented variables as policy instruments.

Table 5.10 shows the distribution of households without various services, by city size and by location relative to the nearest point of supply. The unit of measurement used is an urban block, which in the case of Colombia is approximately 80 meters. The figures show that for electricity and piped water, more than half of these households are located less than a block from a neighbor with the service; for sewerage, it is true for one-fifth of the households.

There are strong differences when households are stratified by city size. The percentage of households that are near the supply network is substantially higher in small towns than in large cities. This means that in small towns either demand factors are more important in explaining absence of consumption or public utility companies are less responsive in providing the connection even when the service is demanded.

Attempts were made to derive information on the reasons for lack of consumption. The head of household was asked to give the most important reason for not having a service in 1974. Table 5.11 shows the distribution of answers for households when the nearest neighbor with the service was less than a block away: that is, for those households where distance from the network was not the obvious limiting factor.

As seen by these households, the most important reason for not having a service is its cost. For electricity and water, if the second and third answers are aggregated, more than two-thirds of the households reported the cost of the service, either in itself or relative to the cost of substitutes, as the main reason for not having the service. For sewerage the percentage is more than half.

The percentage is significantly larger for electricity than for the other services. Because electricity has the largest coverage, this could reflect the fact that households without this service have a lower per capita income than households lacking other services.

Table 5.10. *Distribution of Urban Households without Services in 1974, Classified by Distance from Neighbor with Service*
(percentage)

Distance from nearest neighbor with service (blocks)	Large cities	Inter- mediate cities	Small towns	Urban average
Electricity				
Less than 1	57.4	55.5	79.8	73.4
1 to 3	1.0	10.0	9.2	8.8
More than 3	41.6	34.5	11.0	17.8
Piped water				
Less than 1	45.3	37.0	67.1	54.1
1 to 3	16.9	11.2	9.3	11.5
More than 3	37.8	51.8	23.6	34.4
Sewerage				
Less than 1	16.5	17.1	28.8	22.4
1 to 3	12.8	10.8	10.4	11.1
More than 3	70.7	72.1	60.8	66.5

Table 5.11. *Distribution of Reasons Why Urban Households Are without the Service When There Is a Neighbor with the Service Less Than One Block Away*
(percentage)

Reasons for no connection	Elec- tricity	Piped water	Sewerage
Legal status	5.1	5.4	7.6
Service too expensive	70.8	56.4	47.3
Cheaper substitutes	1.0	8.9	5.8
Request not answered	3.4	3.6	5.8
Network too far	0	1.0	3.4
Complexity of application	3.4	4.5	3.4
Request in process	8.6	7.9	10.4
Other reasons	7.7	12.3	16.3

Table 5.12 classifies households without services according to the substitutes used. Half of the households without direct piped water purchase water from other dwellings. When these particular households were further classified by the reason for no connection,

Table 5.12. *Distribution of Urban Households without the Service, Classified by the Substitute Used*
(percentage)

Piped water	
Well with pump	3.0
Well without pump	20.5
Public standpipe	20.5
Private vendors (trucks)	4.3
Purchased from other dwellings	47.4
Others	4.3
Electricity	
Kerosene lamps	59.0
Candle	41.0
Waste disposal	
Septic tank	21.8
Latrine	44.3
Without any service	33.9

53 percent of them answered that the service was too expensive. The result is of interest; although these households do pay for water, they perceive the present cost as lower than the long-run cost of obtaining the water by direct connection. The reason for this is the high (fixed) cost of connection relative to household consumption and because of the high economies of scale that can be achieved by several households using a single connection.

Public Services and Substitutes in Rural Areas

Table 5.13 presents data on rural families, classified by type of service being used by the household and by income quintile in the rural distribution of income. The percentage of households connected to aqueducts of potable water is 19.9, and the figure is larger for households of higher per capita income. Most of the rural population obtains water directly from wells or rivers without the help of a pumping system.

A stronger relation between income and the availability of service is found for electricity and sewerage, although the negative

Table 5.13. *Sources of Services Used by Rural Households, Classified by Income Quintile in the Distribution of Rural Income* (percentage)

Income quintile (poorest to richest)	From aqueduct	From well or river		From other dwellings	Other
		Without pump	With pump		
Water					
1	15.3	71.7	0.8	3.2	9.0
2	17.2	63.7	0.7	3.7	14.7
3	18.1	60.3	3.2	2.3	16.1
4	25.8	56.1	2.5	1.0	14.5
5	23.3	54.1	6.7	2.1	13.8
Average	19.9	61.2	2.8	2.5	13.6

	Electricity (public)	Kerosene	Candle
Light			
1	8.0	61.5	30.5
2	10.8	50.8	38.4
3	16.0	43.0	41.0
4	15.0	40.2	44.8
5	20.6	41.7	37.7
Average	14.2	47.4	38.4

	Sewerage	Septic tank	Latrine	None
Waste disposal				
1	2.1	4.8	22.1	71.0
2	3.1	6.0	23.2	67.7
3	6.4	9.2	20.2	64.2
4	6.9	7.9	28.6	56.6
5	7.1	9.7	23.0	60.2
Average	5.1	7.5	23.4	64.0

Note: Percentages add to 100 across rows.

welfare implication of a lack of sewerage in low-density rural areas is not obvious.

Probabilities of having and demanding electricity

The probability of having electricity as well as the probability of demanding the service was estimated. This was not done for

Table 5.14. *Regression Coefficient for the Probability of Having Electricity in Rural Areas*

Explanatory variables	Probability of having the service (P)	Probability of demanding the service (P^d)
Constant	0.27	0.91
	(2.5)	(3.3)
Dirt floor	−0.20	−0.24
	(10.5)	(4.5)
Farmers 1	−0.09	−0.06
	(4.3)	(1.4)
Farmers 2	−0.17	−0.40
	(5.2)	(4.1)
Log of per capita income	0.10	0.06
	(5.2)	(1.5)
Log of years of schooling	0.09	0.07
	(2.5)	(1.1)

Note: Values in parentheses show the t-statistic.

the other services, because the differences in the quality of services prevent comparison across households (for example, direct connection to a potable water aqueduct relative to a connection through a system of canals). Moreover, in the rural areas, accessibility to the service is probably more a function of institutional constraints than a result of household behavior.

Table 5.14 shows the results of estimating P and P^d for electricity in the rural areas of Colombia. Dirt floor, per-capita-income, years-of-schooling, and occupational-status-of-head-of-household are significant variables. In this table farmers are defined as households who live on the plots they cultivate: Farmers 1 are owners or tenants of the plot, and Farmers 2 are sharecroppers. They represent, respectively, 51 and 11 percent of the households living in the rural areas. The remaining 38 percent of households are defined as nonfarmers and are wage labor and individuals living in rural areas but not directly engaged in agricultural activities.

The results for P are: (a) dirt floor has a negative coefficient, but less negative than in urban areas; (b) per-capita-income has a coefficient as large as that for small towns in the urban regressions; and (c) the coefficient for small farmers is negative, particularly

Table 5.15. *Rural Households That Became Connected to the Electricity Network between 1970 and 1974*
(percentage)

Income quintile (poorest to richest)	As a percentage of all households that became connected	As a percentage of households without the service in 1970
1	17.7 (31.1)	3.1 (23.0)
2	11.1 (28.4)	1.9 (20.0)
3	31.1 (9.4)	5.6⎫
4	22.2 (13.5)	4.0⎬(16.0)
5	17.7 (17.6)	3.9⎭
Total/average	100.0(100.0)	3.7 (18.0)

Note: Similar figures for the urban area from Tables 5.7 and 5.8 are given in parentheses.

for sharecroppers. It means that farmers have a lower probability of enjoying a particular service than nonfarmers.

In estimating P^d, households on the supply schedule were defined as both those with electricity and those without but with a neighbor less than 100 meters away having it. They represented 88 percent of the total number of households in rural areas.

The Farmers 2 variable has a significantly different coefficient in the regressions for P and P^d. In estimating P, the coefficient is -0.17, but in P^d it is -0.40. This reflects a large difference in the demand for services between the two types of farmers, even when the effects of other variables are held constant.

Changes in the availability of electricity between 1970 and 1974

Which income groups in rural Colombia received electricity services between 1970 and 1974? The first column of Table 5.15 shows that most of the households that received the service—31.1 percent—belong to the third income quintile in the rural income distribution. Only 28.8 percent of the households that received the service belonged to the poorest 40 percent of rural households. The percentage was 59.5 for the poorest 40 percent in urban areas.

The number of households connected in the period expressed as a percentage of those without services in 1970 appears for each income quintile in the second column of Table 5.15. Only 3.7 percent of the rural households without electricity in 1970 received the

Table 5.16. *Rural Households without Electricity,*
Classified by the Distance to the Nearest Neighbor with the Service
(percentage)

	Distance (meters)	Percentage of households
	Less than 100	2.3
	100 to 500	5.2
	500 to 1,000	3.5
	Over 1,000	89.0

service between 1970 and 1974; for the urban areas, the figure was 18 percent. Not only does the rural area have a smaller coverage of the service, but the change in that coverage relative to the initial deficit is also smaller than in urban areas.

Attempts to estimate the probability of rural households having received the service between 1970 and 1974, II, yielded the following result:

$$(10) \quad \text{II} = 0.09 + 0.03 \text{ Log income}$$
$$\phantom{(10) \quad \text{II} = } (2.6) \quad (2.6)$$

$$- 0.08 \text{ Farmer} - 0.09 \text{ Dirt floor,}$$
$$(4.4) \phantom{\text{Farmer} -} (6.8)$$

where, as before, farmers are defined as households living on the same plots they cultivate. In this case, income becomes significant (it was not in the urban area), and the probability becomes positively associated with income. The probability tends to be significantly smaller for farmers than for nonfarmers.

The data on the distribution of households without electricity according to their distance from the network (Table 5.16) show that further connection requires substantial investment in distribution. For 89 percent of these households the nearest neighbor with the service is located more than one kilometer away.

Appendix. Transfers between Urban Consumers Resulting from the Tariff Structure

In Colombia, tariffs for electricity and water vary sharply between residential and nonresidential (industrial and commercial) users, the tariffs for the latter being substantially higher. Moreover, the level of residential tariffs differs markedly across cities.

Residential electricity tariffs are characterized by prices per kilowatt-hour that increase in blocks with additional consumption. Residential water tariffs consist of two components: a fixed charge per month for consumption up to a certain level and a price per cubic meter of additional consumption above that level. The fixed charge increases with the assessed property value of the dwelling. The price per cubic meter is, with a few exceptions, independent of the property value and increases in blocks with increased consumption.

Relation of subsidies and tariffs

The association of property values and consumption levels with household income suggests that tariffs may have induced subsidies and transfers among consumers classified by income groups.

The subsidy received by a household in any income group (i) can be written as:

$$(11) \qquad S_i = (MC - t_i)Q_i,$$

where MC is the long-run marginal cost of providing one unit of the service, t_i is the tariff charged per unit to the ith income group, and Q_i is the amount of the service consumed per unit of time.

The subsidy (S_i) can be divided into two components: the subsidy derived from charging the income group a particular tariff below the mean tariff $(\bar{t})$ and the subsidy received by having a mean tariff below the long-run cost.

$$(12) \qquad S_i = (\bar{t} - t_i)Q_i + (MC - \bar{t})Q_i.$$

The subsidy as a fraction of the household's income (Y) can be written as:

$$(13) \qquad s_i = \frac{(\bar{t} - t_i)}{t_i} \frac{Q_i t_i}{Y} + \frac{(MC - \bar{t})}{t_i} \frac{Q_i t_i}{Y}$$

$$(14) \qquad s_i = \left(\frac{\bar{t}}{t_i} - 1\right)\alpha_i + \frac{\bar{t}}{t_i}\left(\frac{MC}{\bar{t}} - 1\right)\alpha_i,$$

where α_i is the share of income being spent at present in the consumption of the service.

If $MC = \bar{t}$, the subsidy received by a consumer is financed by another consumer paying a tariff higher than the average. In this case, the tariff policy basically generates transfers across consumers or transfers within the system. If $MC > \bar{t}$, the system as a whole is being subsidized: consumers with $t_i < \bar{t}$ get an additional subsidy, and consumers with $t_i > \bar{t}$ may also get a subsidy.

Earlier estimates of the subsidy

Some earlier estimates of the first component of the subsidy are reviewed here. As expected, the main empirical problem in these estimations is to locate the group of households, for which t_i has been computed, in the distribution of income of the country or the particular city in question.

The most comprehensive estimates are those undertaken by Martha Gutierrez de Gomez in a study done at Colombia's National Tariff Bureau for Public Services.[12] Gutierrez de Gomez computed the tariffs paid by consumers in 1974, classified by categories of assessed property values, and then used the 1970 household survey (DANE) to derive property values for different income groups from the actual or imputed rent paid by households. This allowed her to map the distribution of households according to property values on the distribution of income for 1970.

In Table 5.17, the estimated subsidies, as a percentage of household income, are shown for several cities. They differ markedly between cities, with the highest subsidy being received by the poorest 50 percent of households consuming electricity in Medellín. On the average, consumers belonging to the richest quintile tend to finance poorer consumers, particularly those in the middle quintiles.

These distributions of consumers refer to households that were actually billed by utility companies. Households purchasing water or electricity from other dwellings (hooking up among dwellings) as well as households consuming free of charge (consumption from standpipes or illegal connection to transmission lines) are not included. These households do receive subsidies and probably belong to the poorest group among the population.

---

12. Martha Gutierrez de Gomez, *Política Tarifaria y Distribución de Ingresos,* Junta Nacional de Tarifas de Servicios Públicos, 1975 (processed).

Table 5.17. *Subsidies Out of the Tariff Policy as a Percentage of Household's Income, 1970*

(percentage)

Deciles of the population in each city (poorest to richest)	Bogotá Water	Bogotá Electricity	Cali Water	Cali Electricity	Medellín Water	Medellín Electricity
1	—	0.2	—	0.2	—	1.3
2	—	0.4	0.8	0.2	0.5	1.6
3	—⎱ 2.1ᵃ	0.3	0.5⎱ 0.6ᵃ	0.2	0.9	2.1
4	0.9⎰	0.3	0.5⎰	0.2	0.7	2.4
5	0.7⎱ 1.2ᵃ	0.3	0.3⎱ 0.3ᵃ	0.2	0.4	2.0
6	0.5⎰	0.2	0.2⎰	0.2	0.3	1.6
7	0.4⎱ 0.3ᵃ	0.2	−0.2⎱ −0.1ᵃ	—	—	1.3
8	0.2⎰	—	−0.2⎰	—	—	1.0
9	−0.2⎱ −0.6ᵃ	−0.1	−0.1⎱ −0.1ᵃ	—	−0.4	−0.3
10	−0.8⎰	−0.1	−0.7⎰	−0.6	−0.5	−0.2

a. Estimates from Lars Lundquist, "Water and Sewerage Tariffs as a Mean for Income Redistribution in Colombia," memorandum (Washington, D.C.: World Bank, October 23, 1973).
Source: Martha Gutierrez de Gomez, *Política Tarifaria y Distribución de Ingresos.*

The difference between officially billed consumers and actual consumers might explain the differences between Table 5.17 and Tables SA-27, SA-29, and SA-31 in the statistical appendix, which report the percentage of consumers in each quintile according to the 1974 sample survey. For water, Table 5.17 does not report officially billed consumers belonging to the poorest decile. For Bogotá, none are reported in the poorest quintile. Table SA-29 shows that 87 percent of households in the poorest quintile of large cities consumed piped water.

Lars Lundquist, formerly with the World Bank, undertook some estimates of the subsidy from water consumption for 1973.[13] His estimates for Bogotá for the second and third quintile are 2.1 and 1.2 percent, respectively—substantially higher than the estimates of Gutierrez de Gomez.[14] The difference is not so much a

13. Lars Lundquist, "Water and Sewerage Tariffs as a Mean for Income Redistribution in Colombia," memorandum (Washington, D.C.: World Bank, October 23, 1973).
14. Part of the difference results from using different concepts of *t*. Gutierrez de Gomez defines *t* as the average residential tariff, whereas Lundquist defines it by including commercial and industrial consumers, yielding a higher value for *t*.

result of differences in the estimated absolute subsidy (S_i) as of differences in the household income figures used, which in turn result from the difficulty of mapping the distribution of consumers according to property value categories into a distribution according to income levels.

In the case of water, there is evidence that the average tariff falls short of any reasonable estimate for the long-run cost.[15] Defining this cost as the sum of the operating cost, depreciation, and an 8 percent return on net fixed assets (evaluated at reproduction cost), the shortfall ranges from 22 percent for Medellín to 50 percent for Bogotá.[16]

What is the additional subsidy (the second component described earlier) that a typical household in the second and third quintile would receive? With a value of $\alpha_i = 0.015$ and values of t_i/t between one-half and two-thirds (implicit in the Gutierrez de Gomez estimates for these quintiles), the percentage subsidy can be computed as shown below.

Fraction shortfall $(MC - t)/MC$	$\dfrac{MC}{t}$	Share spent, α	Subsidy $= (t/t_i)\left[\dfrac{MC}{t} - 1\right]\alpha_i$	
			$(t_i/t) = 1/2$	$(t_i/t) = 2/3$
0.22	1.28	0.015	0.008	0.006
0.50	2.00	0.015	0.030	0.022

For shortfalls of 0.22, the additional subsidy ranges between six-tenths and eight-tenths of 1 percent of income, a figure similar to that derived for the first concept of subsidy. For shortfalls like that of Bogotá (0.50), the additional subsidy becomes substantially larger: it can range between 2 and 3 percent of income—several times higher than the first concept of subsidy resulting from transfers across consumers.

---

15. See Johannes F. Linn, "The Distributive Effect of Local Government Finances in Colombia: A Review of Evidence," World Bank Staff Working Paper no. 235 (Washington, D.C.: World Bank, March 1976).
   16. Ibid.

Chapter 6

The Distribution of Beneficiaries
of Other Services

THE SAMPLE SURVEY PROVIDED statistically significant information
on the consumption of other services: agricultural loans to farmers
provided by the Caja Agraria, adult retraining courses offered by
the Servicio Nacional de Aprendizaje (SENA), educational fellowships offered by public agencies, and garbage collection services
provided in urban areas. This chapter presents the distribution of
the beneficiaries of these services classified by income groups.

Agricultural Loans by the Caja Agraria, 1974

The Caja Agraria is the major public agency channeling credit
to the agricultural sector at interest rates lower than those charged
by private banks. The Caja tries especially to reach small farmers,
lending conditions being different for farmers with different asset
values.

Implicit subsidy provided by the loans

Approximately 75 percent of the value of loans of the Caja are
for short-term loans, one year or less; the rest are for one to six
years. In 1974, the Caja's interest rates ranged from 14 to 18
percent, depending on the value of the assets of the farmer. Interest rates charged by the private banking system fluctuated
around 25 percent.

New loans extended by the Caja Agraria during 1974 amounted

to 4,449 million pesos.[1] By assuming an average lending term of one year at 16 percent and an alternative market rate of 25 percent, the grant component becomes $1 - (1 + 0.16)/(1 + 0.25)$ or approximately 7.2 percent. If this component is multiplied by the volume of lending, the result is a subsidy of 320 million pesos.[2]

The figure of 7.2 percent is an average; clearly the grant component is quite sensitive to the term of a particular loan. For example, using the earlier interest rate figures, loans of six months and three years would have grant components of 4 and 20 percent, respectively. If small farmers receive shorter-term loans, the grant component tends to be smaller for them.[3]

The foregoing calculations assume that without loans from the Caja, all farmers could obtain credit at the market rate of 25 percent charged by commercial banks. In fact, poor farmers find it difficult or impossible to obtain credit from commercial banks. Given the excess demand that results from charging a low real interest (the nominal rate of 25 percent is legally fixed), credit must somehow be rationed.[4] Thus, poor farmers usually resort to intermediaries charging much higher rates than commercial banks. In rural Colombia, the rates charged by lenders and other informal intermediaries have ranged between 30 and 50 percent a year. Small farmers also obtain credit by selling their crops at prices substantially below the going rate.

---

1. World Bank, "Economic Position and Prospects of Colombia," vol. II, report no. 1548 (a restricted-circulation document) (Washington, D.C., 1977; processed).

2. In computing the grant component of a one-year loan, the following definitions can be used: L = value of the loan; r_1 = concessionary or subsidized interest rate; r_2 = market or alternative interest rate; R_1 = repayment at the end of the year at the concessionary rate, r_1, $R_1 = (1 + r_1)L$; V = present value of R_1, discounted at the alternative or market rate r_2, $V = R_1/(1 + r_2)$.

The grant component, g, can be defined as:

$$g = \frac{L - V}{L} = 1 - \frac{V}{L} = 1 - \frac{R_1/(1 + r_2)}{R_1/(1 + r_1)} = 1 - \left[\frac{1 + r_1}{1 + r_2}\right].$$

If both r_1 and r_2, the concessionary rate and the market rate, are different for farmers of different income or asset levels, the value of g will differ for different farmers. If for poorer farmers r_1 is smaller and r_2 is larger, the grant component g will tend to be higher.

3. This will be true if poorer and smaller farmers tend to get credit for crop production, whereas larger farmers get a higher share of credit for cattle raising.

4. With inflation at 20 percent, the commercial interest rate of 25 percent is equivalent to a 5 percent real rate of interest.

Table 6.1. *Estimates of the Implicit Subsidy Received by Farmers from Loans by the Caja Agraria, 1974*

	Distribution of farmers and aggregate loan			Estimates of the subsidy		
Income quintile (poorest to richest)	*Distribution of farmers (percentage)*	*Distribution of aggregate loan (percentage)*	*Loan to each farmer (L) (pesos[a])*	*Alternative interest rate (percentage)*	*Grant (g) (percentage)*	*Estimated subsidy to each farmer (g.L) (pesos)*
1	34.6	19.6	4,374	40–60	17–28	743–1,224
2	29.3	43.0	11,385	30–50	11–23	1,241–2,595
3	19.5	20.2				
4	12.1	12.5	7,965[b]	25[b]	7[b]	557[b]
5	4.5	4.7				

a. The standard deviation, σ_x, and the sample size, n, are:

$x = 4,374$, $\sigma_x = 2,893$, $n = 43$; $x = 11,385$, $\sigma_x = 13,452$, $n = 34$; $x = 7,965$, $\sigma_x = 9,810$, $n = 53$.

b. Because of the small sample size, the value for farmers in quintiles 3, 4, and 5 was computed as an average of the three quintiles.

Distribution of the subsidy

The 1974 sample survey provided data on 130 farmers who received new loans from the Caja during 1974. The distribution of these farmers in the country distribution of income, the mean loan received, and an estimate of the implicit subsidy appear in Table 6.1. One-third of the farmers who received loans belong to the poorest quintile in the country distribution of income. Almost two-thirds belong to the poorest 40 percent of households.

The second column of Table 6.1 shows the distribution of new credit to farmers by income groups in 1974. Since the mean loan in the richest three quintiles is similar to the average loan, the distribution of the total credit going to these quintiles is almost the same as the distribution of farmers. This is not true for the poorest quintiles; farmers in the first quintile, although more numerous, receive half the share of the total credit received by farmers in the second quintile.

The third column of the table shows figures on the mean loan to each farmer. Because of the small sample size, the value for farmers in quintiles 3, 4, and 5 was computed as an average for the three quintiles. Farmers in quintile 2 received an average

Table 6.2. *Income Distribution of Farmers, 1974*
(percentage)

Income quintile (poorest to richest)	All farmers	Farmers receiving loans from the Caja
1	28.3	34.6
2	26.5	29.3
3	22.0	19.5
4	17.3	12.1
5	5.9	4.5

Note: In the sample survey, farmer is defined as any rural household living on a plot under cultivation and actively involved as landlord, tenant, or sharecropper.

loan of 11,285 pesos ($409), substantially larger than the average loan of 7,695 pesos ($279) reported by all farmers.

The last three columns present a rough estimate of the implicit subsidy to each farmer from each loan. The first column shows a hypothetical range of interest rates from sources other than the Caja; the second, the range of the grant component for a one-year loan; and the third, the range of the implicit subsidy to each farmer. The estimates of the subsidy are for farmers who effectively received a loan and does not represent an average for all farmers in that quintile. In this respect these figures cannot be compared directly to the mean subsidies to each quintile estimated for education and health.

Finally, the income distribution of farmers who received loans from the Caja is compared with the income distribution of all farmers in Table 6.2. Although 28.3 percent of all farmers belong to the poorest (country) quintile, that quintile accounts for 34.6 percent of those farmers who received loans from the Caja.

SENA Training Courses, 1974

Servicio Nacional de Aprendizaje (SENA) is a decentralized public agency in charge of training programs for workers already employed in the private sector. It is financed by a tax on the payroll of enterprises belonging to the urban formal, or modern,

Table 6.3. *Attendance at* SENA *Courses, 1974*
(percentage)

Income quintile (poorest to richest)	Number of students	Man-months of attendance
1	12.7	11.3
2	14.7	11.9
3	24.5	24.3
4	18.9	20.0
5	29.2	32.5

sector: that is, firms whose workers are affiliated with the Social Security System. These enterprises select employees to be trained at SENA on a part-time or full-time basis. During 1974, SENA's expenditures were 628 million pesos, most of which was contributed by the private sector.[5]

In the 1974 sample survey, 377 individuals reported having participated in SENA courses during that year; information on the number of months attended per individual was also reported. Table 6.3 shows the distribution of individuals as well as the distribution of total man-months of attendance, classified according to quintiles in the country distribution of income.

The table shows that about 30 percent of those attending SENA courses belong to the richest quintile in the country income distribution, and most belong to the three richest quintiles. Participants from the poorest 40 percent of families account for only 23 percent of the total man-months of attendance. The smaller representation of the low-income groups can be explained by two factors. First, SENA mainly trains individuals in urban areas (93 percent of the total attendance in 1974 was by urban workers), and urban households are better off than rural households in terms of the country distribution of income. Second, within the urban area, SENA favors workers employed in the modern sector, that is, the best paid labor in the urban sector.

5. Contraloría General de la República de Colombia, *Informe Financiero de 1974.*

Educational Fellowships from Public Agencies, 1974

In the sample survey, seventy-four households reported having received educational fellowships from public agencies during 1974. The (expanded) distribution of these households according to income quintiles is:

Income quintile (poorest to richest)	Percentage of households
1	16.2
2	23.8
3	9.7
4	27.0
5	23.3

The distribution does not show a clear pattern across income quintiles, which is expected in view of the relatively small sample size. A more aggregate interpretation of the data suggests that approximately half of the households that received fellowships belong to the lower 40 percent and the other half to the richest 60 percent.

Garbage Collection Services in Urban Areas, 1974

The 1974 sample survey collected data on the number of urban households with public garbage collection services in 1974.[6] Table 6.4 presents the distribution of these households according to quintiles in the country income distribution.

More than one-third of those with the service belong to the richest quintile, whereas 9.7 percent belong to the poorest. To show the extent to which this is a function of the fraction of urban households in the higher-income quintiles, the distribution of all urban households is given in parentheses according to country quintiles.

6. Data on this service were reported earlier to estimate the probability of having the service. Here only data on households that receive the service and their distribution by income group are given.

Table 6.4. *Urban Households with Garbage Collection Service,*
1974

(percentage)

Income quintile (poorest to richest)	Large cities	Intermediate cities	Small towns	Urban average
1	7.2(9.0)	8.7(12.3)	19.3(29.3)	9.7(15.1)
2	10.0(13.1)	13.6(16.0)	20.8(24.9)	12.9(16.8)
3	16.1(17.4)	17.6(18.1)	19.9(18.5)	17.3(17.8)
4	23.9(23.4)	25.2(25.6)	22.8(16.7)	24.1(22.4)
5	42.8(37.1)	34.9(28.0)	17.1(10.6)	36.0(27.9)

Note: Figures in parentheses show the distribution of all urban households.

Although 27.9 percent of all urban households belong to the richest quintile, their share in the distribution of the service is 36 percent; 15.1 percent of urban households belong to the poorest quintile, and their share in the service is only 9.7 percent. The distribution favors higher-income groups not only because garbage disposal is primarily an urban service, but also because there is a bias in favor of higher-income households within urban areas.

Statistical Appendix

Table SA-1. *Distribution of Families, by per Capita Income, According to the Official Exchange Rate, 1974*
(percentage)

Annual per capita income (dollars)	Small towns	Inter- mediate cities	Large cities	Urban average	Rural areas	Country average
0–50	12.6	3.7	3.7	5.9	10.5	7.6
51–75	14.0	6.8	4.1	7.4	13.6	9.7
76–100	11.5	6.8	5.8	7.5	12.9	9.5
101–150	19.5	15.5	12.3	15.1	23.0	18.0
151–250	20.3	21.5	21.1	21.1	23.0	21.8
251–350	9.6	15.5	12.6	12.6	9.4	11.4
351–500	5.2	9.2	12.7	9.8	4.5	7.8
501–700	2.4	7.3	9.2	6.9	1.5	4.9
701–1,500	3.9	10.2	12.5	9.7	1.2	6.5
Over 1,500	1.0	3.5	6.0	4.0	0.4	2.7
Mean income	176	321	420	326	149	256

Table SA-2. *Distribution of Families, by per Capita Income, According to the Kravis Parity Exchange Rate, 1974*
(percentage)

Annual per capita income (dollars)	Small towns	Inter- mediate cities	Large cities	Urban average	Rural areas	Country average
0–50	3.2	0.2	1.1	1.4	1.9	1.6
51–75	2.8	1.3	1.7	1.9	3.6	2.6
76–100	5.1	1.4	0.7	2.0	4.1	2.8
101–150	11.9	5.9	3.0	6.0	11.4	8.0
151–250	25.1	14.9	10.9	15.6	25.0	19.0
251–350	13.7	12.8	12.2	12.7	18.7	15.0
351–500	14.6	15.9	15.1	15.2	16.9	15.8
501–700	9.7	15.3	13.3	13.0	9.9	11.8
701–1,500	9.0	18.6	23.6	18.5	7.0	14.2
Over 1,500	4.9	13.7	18.4	13.7	1.5	9.2
Mean income	373	681	890	692	317	544

Table SA-3. *Mean Number of Rooms Occupied by the Household*

Regional income quintile (poorest to richest)[a]	Small towns	Inter-mediate cities	Large cities	Urban average	Rural areas	Country average
1	2.63 (1.1)	2.83 (1.3)	2.94 (1.7)	2.78 (1.4)	2.15 (1.1)	2.51 (1.3)
2	2.77 (1.3)	3.03 (1.6)	2.95 (1.7)	2.91 (1.5)	2.34 (1.0)	2.58 (1.3)
3	2.79 (1.2)	3.50 (1.8)	3.00 (1.7)	3.12 (1.7)	2.48 (1.4)	2.74 (1.5)
4	3.10 (1.6)	4.05 (2.0)	4.29 (2.0)	3.86 (1.9)	2.30 (1.1)	3.13 (1.7)
5	3.77 (1.8)	4.27 (2.1)	5.24 (2.5)	4.71 (2.3)	2.80 (1.6)	4.40 (2.3)
Country average	3.01 (1.5)	3.54 (1.9)	3.69 (2.2)	3.48 (1.9)	2.41 (1.3)	3.07 (1.8)

Note: Values in parentheses show the standard deviation.
a. Quintiles in the distribution of income in each region or location.

Table SA-4. *Mean Number of Toilets and Latrines in the Dwelling*

Regional income quintile (poorest to richest)[a]	Small towns	Inter-mediate cities	Large cities	Urban average	Rural areas	Country average
1	0.74 (0.5)	0.99 (0.5)	1.05 (0.6)	0.89 (0.6)	0.31 (0.5)	0.59 (0.6)
2	0.92 (0.7)	1.08 (0.5)	1.27 (0.6)	1.11 (0.6)	0.38 (0.7)	0.70 (0.7)
3	0.89 (0.5)	1.12 (0.7)	1.32 (0.7)	1.13 (0.6)	0.40 (0.6)	0.86 (0.7)
4	1.05 (0.6)	1.50 (0.9)	1.68 (0.9)	1.52 (0.8)	0.43 (0.6)	1.01 (0.8)
5	1.29 (0.7)	2.07 (1.1)	2.44 (1.2)	2.11 (1.2)	0.48 (0.7)	1.81 (1.2)
Country average	0.98 (0.6)	1.35 (0.9)	1.56 (1.0)	1.35 (0.9)	0.40 (0.6)	0.99 (0.9)

Note: Values in parentheses show the standard deviation.
a. Quintiles in the distribution of income in each region or location.

Table SA-5. *Mean Number of Persons in the Household*

Regional income quintile (poorest to richest)[a]	Small towns	Inter-mediate cities	Large cities	Urban average	Rural areas	Country average
1	7.23	6.81	6.47	6.61	6.96	6.87
	(2.5)	(2.5)	(2.6)	(2.6)	(2.4)	(2.5)
2	6.45	5.90	5.25	5.97	6.41	5.99
	(2.6)	(2.6)	(2.3)	(2.5)	(2.3)	(2.5)
3	5.68	5.21	5.08	5.12	5.88	5.38
	(2.4)	(2.5)	(2.4)	(2.6)	(2.5)	(2.5)
4	5.09	4.98	4.61	4.91	4.77	4.80
	(2.7)	(2.4)	(2.3)	(2.3)	(2.6)	(2.4)
5	4.40	4.17	4.30	4.19	4.08	4.25
	(2.2)	(2.3)	(2.2)	(2.2)	(2.3)	(2.3)
Country average	5.75	5.40	5.13	5.36	5.63	5.47
	(2.7)	(2.6)	(2.4)	(2.6)	(2.6)	(2.6)

Note: Values in parentheses show the standard deviation.
a. Quintiles in the distribution of income in each region or location.

Table SA-6. *Mean Number of Income Earners in the Household*

Regional income quintile (poorest to richest)[a]	Small towns	Inter-mediate cities	Large cities	Urban average	Rural areas	Country average
1	1.41	1.35	1.26	1.32	1.19	1.24
	(0.9)	(0.7)	(0.6)	(0.8)	(0.8)	(0.8)
2	1.46	1.58	1.46	1.45	1.19	1.37
	(1.0)	(1.0)	(0.8)	(0.8)	(0.7)	(0.9)
3	1.33	1.65	1.61	1.62	1.42	1.52
	(0.7)	(1.0)	(1.0)	(1.0)	(1.0)	(1.0)
4	1.67	1.55	1.67	1.60	1.42	1.59
	(1.1)	(1.0)	(1.1)	(1.0)	(1.1)	(1.0)
5	1.62	1.66	1.95	1.82	1.58	1.72
	(0.9)	(0.8)	(1.1)	(1.0)	(1.7)	(1.0)
Country average	1.50	1.56	1.60	1.56	1.36	1.48
	(0.9)	(0.9)	(1.0)	(0.9)	(1.0)	(0.9)

Note: Values in parentheses show the standard deviation.
a. Quintiles in the distribution of income in each region or location.

Table SA-7. *Mean Number of Children Age 0 to 5 in the Household*

Regional income quintile (poorest to richest)[a]	Small towns	Inter-mediate cities	Large cities	Urban average	Rural areas	Country average
1	1.31 (1.2)	1.10 (1.2)	1.11 (1.2)	1.17 (1.2)	1.55 (1.3)	1.39 (1.2)
2	1.09 (1.1)	0.90 (1.0)	0.77 (0.9)	0.92 (1.0)	1.36 (1.2)	1.05 (1.1)
3	0.89 (1.1)	0.60 (0.8)	0.61 (0.8)	0.61 (0.9)	1.02 (1.1)	0.76 (1.0)
4	0.56 (0.8)	0.60 (0.8)	0.38 (0.7)	0.53 (0.8)	0.65 (0.9)	0.54 (0.8)
5	0.41 (0.7)	0.48 (0.7)	0.28 (0.6)	0.33 (0.6)	0.39 (0.8)	0.36 (0.7)
Country average	0.85 (1.1)	0.73 (1.0)	0.63 (0.9)	0.71 (1.0)	1.00 (1.2)	0.82 (1.0)

Note: Values in parentheses show the standard deviation.
a. Quintiles in the distribution of income in each region or location.

Table SA-8. *Mean Number of Children Age 6 to 11 in the Household*

Regional income quintile (poorest to richest)[a]	Small towns	Inter-mediate cities	Large cities	Urban average	Rural areas	Country average
1	1.66 (1.3)	1.41 (1.2)	1.38 (1.3)	1.42 (1.3)	1.66 (1.3)	1.57 (1.3)
2	1.36 (1.3)	0.99 (1.2)	0.97 (1.2)	1.13 (1.2)	1.28 (1.2)	1.14 (1.2)
3	1.10 (1.2)	0.82 (1.1)	0.76 (1.0)	0.80 (1.1)	1.08 (1.1)	0.92 (1.2)
4	0.74 (1.1)	0.74 (1.0)	0.58 (0.9)	0.70 (1.0)	0.73 (1.1)	0.64 (0.9)
5	0.44 (0.8)	0.42 (0.8)	0.37 (0.7)	0.38 (0.7)	0.40 (0.8)	0.44 (0.8)
Country average	1.05 (1.2)	0.87 (1.1)	0.81 (1.1)	0.89 (1.1)	1.04 (1.2)	0.94 (1.2)

Note: Values in parentheses show the standard deviation.
a. Quintiles in the distribution of income in each region or location.

Table SA-9. *Mean Number of Children Age 0 to 11
in the Household*

Regional income quintile (poorest to richest)[a]	Small towns	Intermediate cities	Large cities	Urban average	Rural areas	Country average
1	2.98	2.50	2.48	2.59	3.21	2.96
	(1.9)	(1.9)	(1.7)	(1.9)	(2.0)	(1.9)
2	2.47	1.90	1.74	2.05	2.64	2.19
	(1.9)	(1.6)	(1.4)	(1.5)	(1.7)	(1.6)
3	1.98	1.42	1.37	1.41	2.11	1.68
	(1.6)	(1.4)	(1.2)	(1.4)	(1.7)	(1.5)
4	1.30	1.34	0.96	1.23	1.38	1.18
	(1.4)	(1.3)	(1.3)	(1.3)	(1.5)	(1.3)
5	0.86	0.90	0.66	0.71	0.79	0.80
	(1.1)	(1.2)	(1.0)	(1.0)	(1.3)	(1.1)
Country average	1.90	1.61	1.43	1.60	2.04	1.77
	(1.8)	(1.6)	(1.5)	(1.6)	(1.9)	(1.7)

Note: Values in parentheses show the standard deviation.
a. Quintiles in the distribution of income in each region or location.

Table SA-10. *Mean Number of Persons Age 12 to 16
in the Household*

Regional income quintile (poorest to richest)[a]	Small towns	Intermediate cities	Large cities	Urban average	Rural areas	Country average
1	1.05	1.19	1.00	1.04	1.06	1.05
	(1.2)	(1.2)	(1.2)	(1.2)	(1.1)	(1.1)
2	1.08	0.86	0.66	0.90	0.99	0.93
	(1.2)	(1.0)	(1.0)	(1.1)	(1.1)	(1.1)
3	0.88	0.75	0.65	0.71	0.81	0.71
	(1.1)	(1.0)	(0.9)	(1.0)	(1.0)	(1.0)
4	0.68	0.64	0.60	0.61	0.58	0.60
	(1.1)	(1.0)	(0.9)	(0.9)	(0.9)	(0.9)
5	0.55	0.50	0.41	0.46	0.48	0.49
	(0.9)	(0.8)	(0.7)	(0.8)	(0.8)	(0.8)
Country average	0.85	0.78	0.66	0.74	0.79	0.76
	(1.1)	(1.0)	(1.0)	(1.0)	(1.0)	(1.0)

Note: Values in parentheses show the standard deviation.
a. Quintiles in the distribution of income in each region or location.

Table SA-11. *Mean Number of Pregnancies in the Household*

Regional income quintile (poorest to richest)[a]	Small towns	Intermediate cities	Large cities	Urban average	Rural areas	Country average
1	0.23 (0.5)	0.26 (0.5)	0.25 (0.4)	0.24 (0.5)	0.29 (0.5)	0.26 (0.5)
2	0.23 (0.4)	0.23 (0.4)	0.18 (0.4)	0.21 (0.4)	0.21 (0.4)	0.20 (0.4)
3	0.20 (0.4)	0.18 (0.4)	0.15 (0.4)	0.18 (0.4)	0.21 (0.4)	0.21 (0.4)
4	0.17 (0.4)	0.15 (0.4)	0.15 (0.4)	0.15 (0.4)	0.17 (0.4)	0.14 (0.4)
5	0.12 (0.3)	0.21 (0.5)	0.11 (0.3)	0.14 (0.4)	0.11 (0.3)	0.14 (0.4)
Country average	0.19 (0.4)	0.21 (0.4)	0.17 (0.4)	0.18 (0.4)	0.20 (0.4)	0.19 (0.4)

Note: Values in parentheses show the standard deviation.
a. Quintiles in the distribution of income in each region or location.

Table SA-12. *Mean Age of Head of Household*

Regional income quintile (poorest to richest)[a]	Small towns	Intermediate cities	Large cities	Urban average	Rural areas	Country average
1	50.0 (13.1)	44.6 (12.8)	41.6 (12.7)	44.8 (13.9)	45.0 (13.2)	44.8 (13.5)
2	46.3 (14.6)	44.6 (12.8)	42.1 (14.1)	43.5 (12.9)	43.2 (12.9)	44.3 (13.2)
3	44.4 (13.8)	43.6 (13.9)	42.8 (11.8)	44.2 (13.9)	45.4 (13.6)	44.4 (13.9)
4	45.9 (14.7)	42.2 (13.7)	43.5 (13.2)	44.0 (13.6)	46.0 (14.5)	45.3 (14.2)
5	48.3 (15.4)	44.0 (14.7)	46.9 (15.0)	45.4 (14.7)	47.9 (15.0)	45.2 (14.5)
Country average	46.8 (13.6)	43.8 (13.5)	43.4 (13.8)	44.4 (13.8)	45.4 (13.9)	44.8 (13.9)

Note: Values in parentheses show the standard deviation.
a. Quintiles in the distribution of income in each region or location.

Table SA-13. *Mean Total Years of Schooling*
of the Head of Household

Regional income quintile (poorest to richest)[a]	Small towns	Intermediate cities	Large cities	Urban average	Rural areas	Country average
1	2.03	3.42	3.96	3.03	1.70	2.29
	(1.9)	(2.8)	(2.5)	(2.5)	(1.7)	(2.2)
2	2.46	3.85	4.57	3.74	1.78	2.60
	(2.4)	(2.6)	(2.8)	(2.7)	(1.8)	(2.4)
3	2.90	4.68	5.57	4.48	2.00	3.22
	(2.4)	(3.2)	(3.3)	(2.9)	(2.0)	(2.7)
4	3.67	7.15	6.97	6.41	1.81	4.36
	(2.7)	(3.8)	(4.1)	(3.9)	(1.9)	(3.5)
5	5.78	9.77	9.50	9.04	2.52	7.84
	(4.1)	(4.4)	(4.7)	(4.6)	(2.9)	(4.8)
Country average	3.38	5.77	6.13	5.34	1.96	4.05
	(3.1)	(4.2)	(4.1)	(4.1)	(2.1)	(3.8)

Note: Values in parentheses show the standard deviation.
a. Quintiles in the distribution of income in each region or location.

Table SA-14. *Mean Age of Wife in the Household*

Regional income quintile (poorest to richest)[a]	Small towns	Intermediate cities	Large cities	Urban average	Rural areas	Country average
1	36.8	37.6	35.2	36.8	37.4	37.2
	(11.8)	(11.2)	(11.0)	(11.8)	(11.3)	(11.6)
2	37.5	36.4	34.9	37.5	36.3	37.6
	(12.0)	(11.9)	(10.9)	(12.0)	(10.9)	(11.7)
3	36.9	37.1	35.9	36.9	39.3	37.4
	(12.4)	(13.6)	(10.3)	(12.4)	(12.2)	(12.7)
4	37.9	36.5	39.4	37.9	39.1	38.9
	(12.0)	(11.3)	(12.5)	(12.0)	(13.8)	(13.2)
5	38.3	35.9	39.9	38.3	43.1	38.9
	(13.0)	(12.5)	(13.2)	(13.0)	(14.6)	(13.0)
Country average	37.5	36.7	37.0	37.5	38.8	38.0
	(12.3)	(12.1)	(11.8)	(12.2)	(12.7)	(12.4)

Note: Values in parentheses show the standard deviation.
a. Quintiles in the distribution of income in each region or location.

Table SA-15. *Mean Total Years of Schooling of Wife in the Household*

Regional income quintile (poorest to richest)[a]	Small towns	Inter-mediate cities	Large cities	Urban average	Rural areas	Country average
1	1.31	2.11	2.73	2.05	1.34	1.67
	(1.6)	(2.5)	(2.4)	(2.2)	(1.6)	(1.9)
2	2.07	2.22	3.48	2.59	1.51	1.93
	(2.1)	(2.7)	(3.1)	(2.6)	(1.7)	(2.1)
3	2.00	3.48	3.77	3.15	1.67	2.47
	(2.3)	(3.7)	(3.2)	(3.4)	(1.9)	(2.8)
4	2.80	5.41	4.63	4.77	1.56	3.22
	(3.1)	(4.5)	(4.4)	(4.1)	(2.0)	(3.4)
5	3.96	6.11	7.00	6.10	1.89	5.34
	(4.1)	(5.0)	(5.2)	(5.1)	(2.8)	(5.0)
Country average	2.24	3.86	4.34	3.73	1.59	2.91
	(2.9)	(4.1)	(4.1)	(3.9)	(2.0)	(3.5)

Note: Values in parentheses show the standard deviation.
a. Quintiles in the distribution of income in each region or location.

Table SA-16. *Mean Number of Children Age 6 to 11 Registered in School in the Household*

Regional income quintile (poorest to richest)[a]	Small towns	Inter-mediate cities	Large cities	Urban average	Rural areas	Country average
1	0.92	1.06	0.96	0.88	0.85	0.85
	(1.1)	(1.1)	(1.1)	(1.1)	(1.0)	(1.0)
2	0.78	0.68	0.74	0.83	0.57	0.70
	(1.0)	(1.0)	(1.0)	(1.0)	(0.8)	(0.9)
3	0.71	0.67	0.64	0.61	0.61	0.61
	(0.9)	(1.0)	(0.9)	(1.0)	(0.9)	(0.9)
4	0.48	0.65	0.53	0.61	0.41	0.50
	(0.8)	(1.0)	(0.8)	(0.9)	(0.8)	(0.8)
5	0.37	0.39	0.35	0.34	0.24	0.38
	(0.7)	(0.8)	(0.7)	(0.7)	(0.6)	(0.7)
Country average	0.65	0.68	0.64	0.65	0.54	0.61
	(0.9)	(1.0)	(0.9)	(0.9)	(0.9)	(0.9)

Note: Values in parentheses show the standard deviation.
a. Quintiles in the distribution of income in each region or location.

Table SA-17. *Mean Number of Persons Age 12 to 16 Registered in School in the Household*

Regional income quintile (poorest to richest)[a]	Small towns	Inter-mediate cities	Large cities	Urban average	Rural areas	Country average
1	0.61	0.98	0.83	0.77	0.48	0.62
	(0.9)	(1.1)	(1.1)	(1.0)	(0.8)	(0.9)
2	0.78	0.71	0.55	0.72	0.55	0.61
	(1.0)	(1.0)	(0.9)	(1.0)	(0.9)	(1.0)
3	0.67	0.63	0.56	0.58	0.41	0.50
	(1.0)	(1.0)	(0.9)	(0.9)	(0.8)	(0.9)
4	0.53	0.55	0.55	0.54	0.30	0.47
	(1.0)	(0.9)	(0.8)	(0.9)	(0.6)	(0.8)
5	0.45	0.41	0.34	0.39	0.24	0.41
	(0.8)	(0.8)	(0.7)	(0.7)	(0.6)	(0.8)
Country average	0.61	0.66	0.56	0.60	0.40	0.52
	(1.0)	(1.0)	(0.9)	(0.9)	(0.8)	(0.9)

Note: Values in parentheses show the standard deviation.
a. Quintiles in the distribution of income in each region or location.

Table SA-18. *Number of Teachers in Public Primary Schools, by Category and Stratum, 1973*

Stratum	Without category	Categories				Total
		4 (lowest pay)	3	2	1 (highest pay)	
Bogotá	27	10	84	3,651	4,513	8,285
Cali	33	47	97	949	1,037	2,163
Medellín	10	7	32	300	2,586	2,935
Barranquilla	14	16	26	357	1,256	1,669
5	12	14	21	166	789	1,002
6	39	130	130	344	707	1,350
7	10	94	118	516	1,156	1,894
8	21	11	44	270	854	1,200
9	7	6	48	438	1,412	1,911
10	23	19	90	287	409	828
11	318	155	414	628	1,886	3,401
12	37	19	52	171	642	921
13	6	1	8	139	750	904
14	50	7	25	143	128	353

Table SA-18. (*Continued*)

		Categories				
Stratum	Without category	4 (lowest pay)	3	2	1 (highest pay)	Total
15	50	88	72	324	272	806
16	24	117	49	278	308	776
17	63	59	53	413	583	1,171
18	34	73	60	344	596	1,107
19	30	13	99	452	1,446	2,040
20	16	20	91	384	685	1,196
21	1	5	42	232	662	942
22	156	176	238	545	1,292	2,407
23	123	86	180	317	741	1,447
24	56	67	116	327	602	1,168
25	49	46	108	240	784	1,227
26	39	29	61	432	608	1,169
27	92	47	69	436	717	1,361
28	355	245	166	544	272	1,582
29	1,130	302	190	379	189	2,190
30	543	406	215	578	277	2,019
31	1,121	231	361	513	301	2,527
32	145	65	139	986	1,143	2,478
33	43	80	157	815	1,139	2,234
34	943	151	363	646	537	2,640
35	10	38	63	594	740	1,538
36	—[a]	—[a]	—[a]	—[a]	—[a]	—[a]
37	326	123	129	184	94	856
38	234	81	272	462	378	1,427
39	87	26	120	386	607	1,226
40	100	105	256	716	529	1,706
41	106	22	86	189	164	567
42	763	362	276	668	294	2,363
43	1,756	836	432	932	490	4,446
44	28	14	5	33	9	89
45	194	125	68	341	195	923
46	430	76	134	454	415	1,509
47	134	89	154	531	747	1,655
48	508	36	50	121	125	840

a. No schools outside the cabecera.
Source: COLDATOS report, pp. 16–17.

Table SA-19. *Monthly Wage of Teachers in Public Primary Schools, by Category and Departments, 1973*
(pesos)

Department	Without category	Categories			
		4 (lowest pay)	3	2	1 (highest pay)
Antioquia	1,270	1,540	1,659	1,776	2,052
Atlántico	0	1,526	1,678	1,896	2,256
Bogotá, D. E.	0	2,071	2,125	2,180	2,234
Bolívar	1,206	1,381	1,621	1,903	2,180
Boyacá	1,071	1,542	1,714	1,795	2,048
Caldas	1,287	1,551	1,754	1,859	2,057
Cauca	1,127	1,354	1,487	1,621	1,987
Cesar	1,298	1,628	1,749	1,892	2,090
Córdoba	1,281	1,443	1,576	1,914	2,202
Cundinamarca	1,166	1,628	1,793	1,940	2,123
Chocó	1,265	1,321	1,561	1,740	2,040
Huila	1,038	1,343	1,487	1,665	1,998
La Guajira	1,232	1,831	1,967	2,115	2,245
Magdalena	1,038	1,622	1,804	1,908	2,046
Meta	1,265	1,845	1,610	1,848	2,145
Narino	1,021	1,376	1,510	1,654	1,987
N. Santander	1,239	1,543	1,709	1,889	2,110
Quindío	1,371	1,644	1,694	1,809	2,070
Risaralda	1,298	1,476	1,587	1,665	1,887
Santander	1,077	1,387	1,554	1,776	1,998
Sucre	1,143	1,496	1,703	1,973	2,344
Tolima	1,341	1,496	1,587	1,776	1,998
Valle del Cauca	1,624	1,820	1,853	1,929	2,134
Average	1,229	1,426	1,686	1,849	2,097

Source: COLDATOS report, p. 21.

Table SA-20. *Estimate of the Costs of Public Health Centers, 1974*

Number and costs of centers	Large cities	Inter-mediate cities	Small towns	Rural areas	Country total
		Location of institution			
Number of centers					
With beds	—	—	20	16	36
Without beds	148	139	262	133	682
Cost for each center, 1969[a] (thousands of pesos)					
With beds	—	—	131	100	
Without beds	354	193	93	71	
Estimated cost for each center, 1974[b] (thousands of pesos)					
With beds	—	—	266	203	
Without beds	719	392	189	144	
Cost for all centers, 1974 (millions of pesos)					
With beds	—	—	*5.3*	*3.2*	*8.5*
Without beds	*106.4*	*54.5*	*49.5*	*19.1*	*229.5*
Total	*106.4*	*54.5*	*54.8*	*22.3*	*238.3*

a. COLDATOS report.
b. Adjusted by the change in the price level between 1969 and 1974.

Table SA-21. *Estimate of Subsidy to Each Puesto de Salud, 1974*
(pesos)

Institution	Number of staff	Subsidy
Health center, 1969		
Doctors	1.88	61,275
Auxiliares	3.70	49,788
Total	5.58	111,063
Puesto de salud, 1969		
Doctors	0.53	17,274
Auxiliares	1.06	14,263
Total	1.59	31,537
Total, 1974 pesos		64,020

Source: COLDATOS report.

Table SA-22. *Total Subsidy to Puestos de Salud, 1974*

Number and costs of puestos	Location of institution				
	Large cities	Intermediate cities	Small towns	Rural areas	Country total
Cost of each puesto (pesos)	64,020	64,020	64,020	64,020	64,020
Number of puestos	18	114	539	899	1,570
Subsidy (millions of pesos)	1.2	7.3	34.5	57.5	100.5

Table SA-23. *Number of Services Received in Hospitals of the National Health System as Reported by Households, 1974*
(thousands)

Income quintile (poorest to richest)	Large cities	Inter- mediate cities	Small towns	Urban total	Rural areas	Country total
			Location of household			
Outpatient visits						
1	146	129	312	587	319	906
2	130	183	214	527	333	860
3	164	178	250	592	267	859
4	281	322	116	719	226	945
5	170	228	47	445	59	504
Total	891	1,040	939	2,870	1,204	4,074
Deliveries						
1	9	8	11	28	24	52
2	8	9	7	24	24	48
3	6	7	6	19	16	35
4	8	8	2	18	8	26
5	3	4	4	11	4	15
Total	34	36	30	100	76	176
Operations						
1	12	3	4	19	10	29
2	3	4	2	9	8	17
3	4	8	0	12	3	15
4	12	6	3	21	4	25
5	18	3	2	23	0	23
Total	49	24	11	84	25	109
Inpatient days						
1	743	292	194	1,412	620	2,032
2	232	251	155	455	845	1,300
3	253	157	92	502	719	1,221
4	145	280	87	512	396	908
5	238	100	132	470	99	569
Total	1,611	1,080	660	3,351	2,679	6,030

Table SA-24. *Number of Services Received in Hospitals of the Social Security System* (ICSS *and Cajas*) *as Reported by Households, 1974*
(thousands)

			Location of household			
Income quintile (poorest to richest)	Large cities	Intermediate cities	Small towns	Urban total	Rural areas	Country total
Outpatient visits						
1	33	83	28	144	45	189
2	183	163	146	492	59	551
3	374	203	87	664	70	734
4	418	345	102	865	55	920
5	502	335	48	885	9	894
Total	1,510	1,129	411	3,050	238	3,288
Deliveries						
1	0	2	—	2	3	5
2	3	1	2	6	1	7
3	9	1	3	13	2	15
4	5	6	2	13	3	16
5	5	6	1	12	—	12
Total	22	16	8	46	9	55
Operations						
1	2	1	0	3	—	3
2	3	0	0	3	—	3
3	6	1	1	8	—	8
4	1	2	0	3	—	3
5	4	1	0	5	—	5
Total	16	5	1	22	—	22
Inpatient days						
1	55	12	38	105	—	105
2	128	14	29	171	—	171
3	316	24	20	360	—	360
4	142	170	13	325	—	325
5	137	60	0	197	—	197
Total	778	280	100	1,158	—	1,158

Table SA-25. *Distribution of Public Subsidies to Hospitals of the National Health System* (NHS), *the Social Security System* (SSS), *and Health Centers of All Types* (HC), *1974*
(millions of pesos)

Income quintile (poorest to richest)	Location of household							
	Large cities				Intermediate cities			
	NHS	SSS	HC	Total	NHS	SSS	HC	Total
1	102.0	38.0	15.6	155.6	42.6	16.1	12.2	70.9
2	33.4	92.9	29.9	156.2	41.6	18.5	17.8	77.9
3	38.5	206.6	31.4	276.5	39.3	30.0	11.4	80.7
4	46.2	120.4	20.1	186.7	52.5	87.5	14.3	154.3
5	62.7	154.4	10.6	227.7	23.5	51.7	6.1	81.3
Total	282.8	612.3	107.6	1,002.7	199.5	203.8	61.8	465.1

	Small towns				Urban total			
	NHS	SSS	HC	Total	NHS	SSS	HC	Total
1	40.4	13.4	33.7	87.5	185.0	67.5	61.5	314.0
2	30.0	19.2	26.8	76.0	105.0	130.6	74.5	310.1
3	20.4	24.9	14.5	59.8	98.2	261.5	57.3	417.0
4	18.6	11.2	7.1	36.9	117.3	219.1	41.5	377.9
5	21.7	3.4	7.2	32.3	107.9	209.5	23.9	341.3
Total	131.1	72.1	89.3	292.5	613.4	888.2	258.7	1,760.3

	Rural total				Country total			
	NHS	SSS	HC	Total	NHS	SSS	HC	Total
1	99.5	6.7	24.3	130.5	284.5	74.2	85.8	444.5
2	126.1	8.5	22.2	156.8	231.1	139.1	96.7	466.9
3	103.0	8.4	20.3	131.7	201.2	269.9	77.6	548.7
4	61.8	6.1	9.4	77.3	179.1	225.2	50.9	455.2
5	14.6	1.3	3.6	19.5	122.5	210.8	27.5	360.8
Total	405.0	31.0	79.8	515.8	1,018.4	919.2	338.5	2,276.1

Table SA-26. *Alternate Distribution of Public Subsidies to Hospitals, 1974*

(millions of pesos)

Income quintile (*poorest to richest*)	Location of household							
	Large cities				Intermediate cities			
	NHS	SSS	HC	Total	NHS	SSS	HC	Total
1	46.4	28.2	15.6	90.2	24.7	13.4	12.2	50.3
2	41.3	88.2	29.9	159.4	35.1	32.4	17.8	85.3
3	52.0	113.9	31.4	197.3	34.1	44.6	11.4	90.1
4	89.1	158.0	20.1	267.2	61.8	52.8	14.3	128.9
5	54.0	224.2	10.6	288.8	43.8	60.6	6.1	110.5
Total	282.8	612.3	107.6	1,002.7	199.5	203.8	61.8	465.1
	Small towns				Urban total			
	NHS	SSS	HC	Total	NHS	SSS	HC	Total
1	43.6	10.2	33.7	87.5	114.7	51.8	61.5	228.0
2	29.9	15.6	26.8	72.3	106.3	136.2	74.5	317.0
3	34.9	18.7	14.5	68.1	121.0	177.2	57.3	355.5
4	16.2	15.9	7.1	39.2	167.1	226.7	41.5	435.3
5	6.5	11.7	7.2	25.4	104.3	296.4	23.9	424.6
Total	131.1	72.1	89.3	292.5	613.4	888.2	258.7	1,760.3
	Rural total				Country total			
	NHS	SSS	HC	Total	NHS	SSS	HC	Total
1	107.4	8.5	24.3	140.2	222.1	52.3	85.8	360.2
2	111.8	6.6	22.2	140.6	218.1	142.8	96.7	457.6
3	89.9	8.3	20.3	118.5	210.9	185.5	77.6	474.0
4	76.1	5.4	9.4	90.9	243.2	232.1	50.9	526.2
5	19.8	2.2	3.6	25.6	124.1	298.6	27.5	450.2
Total	405.0	31.0	79.8	515.8	1,018.4	919.2	338.5	2,276.1

Note: The SSS subsidy is classified according to the distribution of affiliated individuals; the NHS subsidy in hospitals is classified according to the distribution of outpatient visits.

Table SA-27. *Percentage of Families with Electricity,*
by Regional Quintiles

Income quintile (poorest to richest)	Large cities	Inter- mediate cities	Small towns	Urban average	Rural areas	Country average
			1974			
1	97.5	90.7	63.2	74.2	8.0	41.4
2	98.3	89.1	70.2	79.3	10.8	49.1
3	99.5	95.4	71.1	88.9	17.7	61.7
4	99.8	98.4	86.4	90.3	15.9	73.5
5	100.0	98.7	94.5	91.3	25.7	91.3
Country average	98.9	94.3	72.4	84.9	15.6	63.2
			1970			
1	92.9	86.9	51.8	75.9	5.3	37.7
2	94.9	87.7	63.6	84.4	9.6	46.0
3	99.1	94.8	69.7	93.3	12.0	58.2
4	99.8	98.2	81.7	98.3	14.3	71.9
5	97.5	98.7	95.4	98.2	19.7	89.9
Country average	96.7	93.1	73.8	89.9	12.0	60.5

Note: Regional quintiles are defined in the distribution of regional income, not country income.

Table SA-28. *Percentage of Families with Electricity,*
by per Capita Household Income

Annual per capita income (dollars)	Large cities	Inter-mediate cities	Small towns	Urban average	Rural areas	Country average
			1974			
0–75	95.8	89.8	59.7	77.4	7.8	41.9
76–150	98.3	88.2	70.4	85.9	14.0	50.8
151–350	99.1	96.2	88.7	95.9	16.1	67.4
351–700	99.8	97.8	100.0	99.3	20.3	87.0
Over 701	100.0	99.0	91.2	98.9	38.1	95.5
Country average	99.0	94.3	75.9	91.9	13.8	62.9
			1970			
0–75	90.0	86.8	54.6	72.7	5.6	38.5
76–150	94.6	85.1	68.7	83.1	11.2	47.5
151–350	97.6	95.7	84.8	94.2	15.3	64.7
351–700	99.8	98.5	100.0	99.5	19.0	86.2
Over 701	97.2	99.0	95.6	97.6	38.9	93.9
Country average	96.7	93.2	72.9	89.7	10.9	60.3

Table SA-29. *Percentage of Families with Piped Water, by Regional Quintiles*

Income quintile (poorest to richest)	Large cities	Inter-mediate cities	Small towns	Urban average	Rural areas	Country average
			1974			
1	87.1	81.3	62.6	77.0	15.3	44.0
2	92.3	85.5	78.7	85.8	17.2	49.5
3	97.3	90.3	79.7	90.9	18.1	62.2
4	99.4	96.1	84.2	96.8	25.8	71.8
5	100.0	96.9	92.7	98.6	23.3	89.0
Country average	95.1	90.1	79.8	89.8	19.9	63.2
			1970			
1	80.6	78.4	57.6	72.5	5.5	36.7
2	89.4	81.9	73.0	81.3	10.7	45.1
3	95.7	89.7	79.7	89.8	12.4	56.4
4	98.8	95.6	80.3	95.8	17.1	69.7
5	97.5	98.5	90.1	97.5	21.2	88.2
Country average	92.3	88.9	76.3	87.3	13.3	59.1

Note: Regional quintiles are defined in the distribution of regional income, not country income.

Table SA-30. *Percentage of Families with Piped Water, by per Capita Household Income*

Annual per capita income (dollars)	Large cities	Inter-mediate cities	Small towns	Urban average	Rural areas	Country average
1974						
0–75	84.1	85.0	64.6	75.2	15.5	44.6
76–150	89.2	81.7	79.9	84.0	16.9	50.6
151–350	96.0	90.9	85.8	92.2	24.8	67.2
351–700	99.5	95.7	96.9	98.2	23.6	84.9
Over 701	100.0	97.6	97.2	99.1	22.9	93.9
Country average	95.1	89.8	79.4	89.7	19.5	62.9
1970						
0–75	80.2	82.4	58.1	70.4	6.2	37.5
76–150	84.1	78.4	78.0	80.4	11.4	46.1
151–350	93.5	89.9	82.3	89.9	18.4	63.4
351–700	98.9	97.1	94.1	97.9	19.4	83.4
Over 701	97.3	98.5	97.2	97.6	31.7	93.1
Country average	92.4	88.8	75.7	87.2	13.1	58.9

Table SA-31. *Percentage of Families with Sewerage,*
by Regional Quintiles

Income quintile (poorest to richest)	Large cities	Inter-mediate cities	Small towns	Urban average	Rural areas	Country average
			1974			
1	80.0	59.7	40.0	58.4	2.1	27.6
2	88.5	73.3	54.4	73.5	3.1	36.6
3	92.1	74.6	60.8	81.7	6.4	48.2
4	96.0	87.2	69.2	90.6	6.9	61.4
5	98.7	90.7	83.9	94.3	7.1	83.3
Country average	90.9	77.2	61.9	79.7	5.1	51.3
			1970			
1	76.3	58.3	32.8	55.3	.8	25.1
2	84.0	69.7	53.3	69.2	2.1	35.1
3	91.7	74.2	54.7	79.6	6.7	45.0
4	94.5	86.3	63.1	88.5	6.3	61.1
5	96.0	89.2	79.9	92.0	9.0	81.7
Country average	88.4	75.6	57.1	76.9	4.9	49.4

Note: Regional quintiles are defined in the distribution of regional income, not country income.

Table SA-32. *Percentage of Families with Sewerage,*
by per Capita Household Income

Annual per capita income (dollars)	Large cities	Inter-mediate cities	Small towns	Urban average	Rural areas	Country average
			1974			
0–75	77.7	64.2	43.3	58.4	1.8	29.4
76–150	83.7	68.2	56.7	70.1	5.0	37.7
151–350	90.8	77.4	74.6	83.0	6.2	54.6
351–700	96.4	87.0	83.1	92.3	10.0	77.6
Over 701	98.6	92.7	83.4	95.5	10.2	89.7
Country average	90.9	77.4	61.3	79.6	5.0	51.2
			1970			
0–75	73.2	58.5	36.9	52.8	1.0	26.2
76–150	80.2	67.0	51.2	67.1	4.5	35.9
151–350	88.8	75.8	68.2	80.2	7.0	53.0
351–700	95.2	85.7	79.2	90.8	9.9	76.4
Over 701	95.5	91.9	83.4	93.4	10.2	87.8
Country average	88.4	75.4	56.3	76.6	4.8	49.2

Table SA-33. *Probability of Having Electricity,*
by per Capita Household Income

Per capita annual household income, 1974 (dollars)[a]	Year	Probability (percentage)			
			Urban areas		
		Rural areas	Small towns	Inter-mediate cities	Large cities
50	1970	4	65	82	93
(115)	1974	12	71	86	97
75	1970	7	70	87	94
(172)	1974	15	75	90	98
100	1970	8	72	89	95
(230)	1974	16	76	92	98
150	1970	10	75	91	96
(345)	1974	18	78	94	98
250	1970	11	76	93	97
(575)	1974	19	79	96	99
350	1970	11	77	94	97
(805)	1974	20	79	96	99
500	1970	11	78	94	97
(1,150)	1974	20	80	97	99
700	1970	12	78	95	98
(1,610)	1974	20	80	97	99
1,500	1970	12	79	95	98
(3,450)	1974	21	81	98	99

Note: Predicted values from the linear probability function.

a. Values in parentheses show the corresponding monthly per capita income in Colombian pesos in December 1974 (to which the coefficients of the regressions apply). The exchange rate used is 27.6 pesos for each dollar.

Table SA-34. *Probability of Having Piped Water,*
by per Capita Household Income

Per capita annual household income, 1974 (dollars)[a]	Year	Probability (percentage)		
		Small towns	Inter-mediate cities	Large cities
50	1970	70	75	82
(115)	1974	73	82	87
75	1970	74	81	87
(172)	1974	77	86	91
100	1970	76	85	89
(230)	1974	79	88	93
150	1970	79	88	91
(345)	1974	81	90	94
250	1970	80	90	93
(575)	1974	83	91	96
350	1970	81	91	94
(805)	1974	83	92	96
500	1970	82	92	95
(1,150)	1974	84	93	97
700	1970	82	93	95
(1,610)	1974	84	93	97
1,500	1970	83	93	96
(3,450)	1974	85	93	98

Note: Predicted values from the linear probability function.

a. Values in parentheses show the corresponding monthly per capita income in Colombian pesos in December 1974 (to which the coefficients of the regressions apply). The exchange rate used is 27.6 pesos for each dollar.

Table SA-35. *Probability of Having Sewerage,*
by per Capita Household Income

Per capita annual household income, 1974 (dollars)[a]	Year	Probability (percent)		
		Small towns	Inter-mediate cities	Large cities
50	1970	48	54	78
(115)	1974	53	58	81
75	1970	53	64	83
(172)	1974	59	67	86
100	1970	56	69	86
(230)	1974	61	72	88
150	1970	59	74	88
(345)	1974	64	76	90
250	1970	61	78	90
(575)	1974	66	80	92
350	1970	63	79	91
(805)	1974	67	82	93
500	1970	63	81	91
(1,150)	1974	68	83	94
700	1970	64	82	92
(1,610)	1974	69	84	92
1,500	1970	64	83	93
(3,450)	1974	69	85	94

Note: Predicted values from the linear probability function.

a. Values in parentheses show the corresponding monthly per capita income in Colombian pesos in December 1974 (to which the coefficients of the regressions apply). The exchange rate used is 27.6 pesos for each dollar.

Table SA-36. *Probability of Having Street Lighting,*
by per Capita Household Income

Per capita annual household income, 1974 (dollars)[a]	Year	Probability (percent)		
		Small towns	Inter-mediate cities	Large cities
50	1970	60	66	89
(115)	1974	73	78	94
75	1970	65	74	91
(172)	1974	76	83	95
100	1970	68	78	93
(230)	1974	78	86	96
150	1970	70	81	95
(345)	1974	80	88	97
250	1970	72	84	96
(575)	1974	81	90	98
350	1970	73	86	97
(805)	1974	82	91	98
500	1970	73	87	97
(1,150)	1974	82	92	98
700	1970	74	87	97
(1,610)	1974	82	92	99
1,500	1970	74	88	98
(3,450)	1974	83	93	99

Note: Predicted values from the linear probability function.

a. Values in parentheses show the corresponding monthly per capita income in Colombian pesos in December 1974 (to which the coefficients of the regressions apply). The exchange rate used is 27.6 pesos for each dollar.

Table SA-37. *Probability of Having Garbage Collection,*
by per Capita Household Income

Per capita annual household income, 1974 (dollars)[a]	Year	Probability (percent)		
		Small towns	Inter-mediate cities	Large cities
50	1970	37	43	69
(115)	1974	37	46	70
75	1970	42	54	75
(172)	1974	43	57	76
100	1970	45	59	78
(230)	1974	47	63	78
150	1970	48	64	81
(345)	1974	51	69	81
250	1970	50	68	83
(575)	1974	54	73	84
350	1970	51	70	84
(805)	1974	55	75	84
500	1970	52	72	85
(1,150)	1974	56	76	85
700	1970	53	73	86
(1,610)	1974	56	78	86
1,500	1970	53	74	86
(3,450)	1974	57	79	86

Note: Predicted values from the linear probability function.

a. Values in parentheses show the corresponding monthly per capita income in Colombian pesos in December 1974 (to which the coefficients of the regressions apply). The exchange rate used is 27.6 pesos for each dollar.

References

The word *processed* indicates works that are reproduced by mimeograph, Xerox, or in a manner other than conventional typesetting and printing.

Berry, Albert, and Miguel Urrutia. *Income Distribution in Colombia*. New Haven: Yale University Press, 1976.

CAJANAL (Caja Nacional de Previsión). "Prestaciones Médicas," *Presupuesto de Ingreso y Rentas.*

CAPRECOM (Caja de Previsión de Comuncaciones). "Servicios Médicos," *Presupuesto de Entidades Decentralizadas, Informe Financiero de 1973, República de Colombia.*

Compañía Colombiana de Datos (COLDATOS). "Design of the Sample of the World Bank Study" ("Diseño de la Muestra del Banco Mundial"). Study prepared for the World Bank, Bogotá, 1976. Processed.

Compañía Colombiana de Datos (COLDATOS). "Unit Cost of Education and Health Services in Colombia in 1974" [Costos Unitarios de los Servicios de Educación y Salud en Colombia en 1974]. Study prepared for the World Bank, Bogotá, 1976. Processed.

Contraloría General de la República de Colombia. "Informe Financiero de 1974." Processed.

DANE (Colombia Bureau of Census). "Household Survey," 1970. Processed.

DANE (Colombia Bureau of Census). "Investigación sobre Establecimientos Educativos," 1972. Processed.

Departmento Nacional de Planeación, Colombia.

"El Sector de Acueducto y Alcantarillados." Documento D.N.P., June 1976.

Gutierrez de Gomez, Martha. *Política Tarifaría y Distribución de Ingresos*, Junta Nacional de Tarifas de Servicios Públicos, 1975. Processed.

ICOLPE (Instituto Colombiano de Pedagogia). "Costos de la Educación Media Oficial," 1972. Processed.

INPES (Instituto para Promgramas Especiales de la Salud), "Censo de Instituciones Hospitalarias," 1970. Processed.

International Financial Statistics.

Jain, Shail. *Size Distribution of Income: A Compilation of Data.* Baltimore: Johns Hopkins University Press, 1975.

Jallade, Jean-Pierre. *Public Expenditures on Education and Income Distribution in Colombia.* World Bank Staff Occasional Papers, no. 18. Baltimore: Johns Hopkins University Press, 1974.

Kravis, Irving B., Zoltan Kenessey, Alan Heston, and Robert Summers. *A System of International Comparisons of Gross Product and Purchasing Power.* Baltimore: Johns Hopkins University Press, 1975.

Linn, Johannes F. "The Distributive Effect of Local Government Finances in Colombia: A Review of Evidence." World Bank Staff Working Paper, no. 235. Washington, D.C.: World Bank, March 1976.

Linn, Johannes F. "Public Utilities in Metropolitan Bogotá: Organization, Service Levels, and Financing," Urban and Regional Economics Division, Development Economics Department. Washington, D.C.: World Bank, May 1976. Processed.

Lundquist, Lars. "Water and Sewerage Tariffs as a Mean for Income Redistribution in Colombia." Memorandum. Washington, D.C.: World Bank, October 23, 1973.

Ministerio de Educación. "Ejecución Presupuestal." Processed.

Ministerio de Educación. "Estadísticas de la Educación Primaria Oficial." Processed.

Ministerio de Educación, ICFES. "La Educación en Cifras, 1970–1974." December 1975. Processed.

Ministerio de Educación. "Oficina Coordinadora de los FER y Oficina de Planeamiento de la Educación." Processed.

Netter, J., and E. Scott Maynes, "On the Appropriateness of the Correlation Coefficient with a 0,1 Dependent Variable." *Journal of the American Statistical Association* (June 1970).

Rama, German. "Origen Social de la Población Universitaria." Universidad Nacional, 3, August 1969. Processed.

Urrutia, Miguel, and Clara E. de Sandoval. "Política Fiscal y Distribución del Ingreso en Colombia," Revista Banco de la República, July 1974.

World Bank. "Economic Position and Prospects of Colombia," vol. II. Report no. 1548. A restricted-circulation document. Washington, D.C., 1977. Processed.

Index

Adult retraining, 6, 35
Age of head of household, 31, 124
Agriculture, public investment in, 33–35; loans for, 143–46

Beneficiaries of services, 5; rural-urban distribution of, 6
Berry, Albert, 8n, 18, 19, 41, 42
Budget, national, 12–13
Bureau of Census, 16, 36–37, 58

Caja Agraria, 7, 35; agricultural loans by, 143–46
Caja Nacional de Previsión (CAJANAL), 77–78
CAJANAL. *See* Caja Nacional de Previsión
Caja de Previsión de Communicaciones (CAPRECOM), 78
Cajas Publicas. *See* Social Security of the Public Sector
CAPRECOM. *See* Caja de Previsión de Communicaciones
COLDATOS. *See* Compañía Columbiana de Datos
Colombian Institute of Social Security (ICSS): costs of, 21; funding for, 77; hospitals under, 83–85, 91; subsidy to, 22–23, 92–93; workers' contributions to, 80–81
Compañía Colombian de Datos (COLDATOS), 14, 50, 57n

Consumption of public services: household versus countrywide survey of, 13–14; inequality in, 4; supply-demand analysis of, 5, 10, 27–33; urbanization and, 14–16
Costs of services, 12; for education, 57–58; for health, 84–88; for ICSS and NHS, 21–22

DANE. *See* Departamento de Estadística
DANE-Polibio Córdoba income distribution study, 43
de Gomez, Martha Gutierrez, 140–42
Demand for services. *See* Supply-demand analysis of public services
Departamento de Estadística (DANE), 16, 36, 62, 73n
de Sandoval, Clara E., 70–72
Dirt floor, and demand for public utility services, 29, 122, 123, 124, 125
Distribution of income. *See* Income distribution

Education: cost of, 12, 57–58; and demand for services, 6, 30; inequality in consumption of, 4; studies on distributive effect of expenditures on, 70–76; and visits to physicians, 98, 99. *See also* Education subsidies; Higher education; Primary education; Secondary education; Student enrollment

The full range of World Bank publications, both free and for sale, is described in the *Catalog of World Bank Publications*, and of the continuing research program of the World Bank, in *World Bank Research Program: Abstracts of Current Studies*. The most recent edition of each is available without charge from:

PUBLICATIONS UNIT
THE WORLD BANK
1818 H STREET, N.W.
WASHINGTON, D.C. 20433
U.S.A.